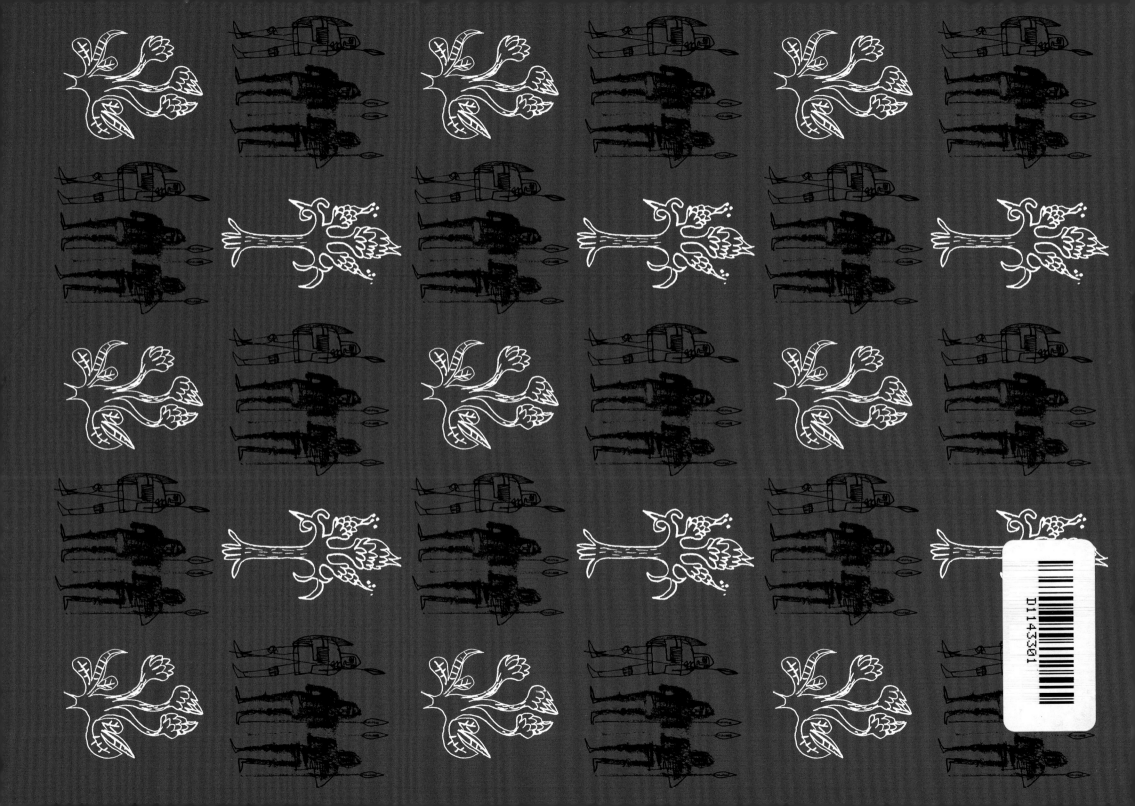

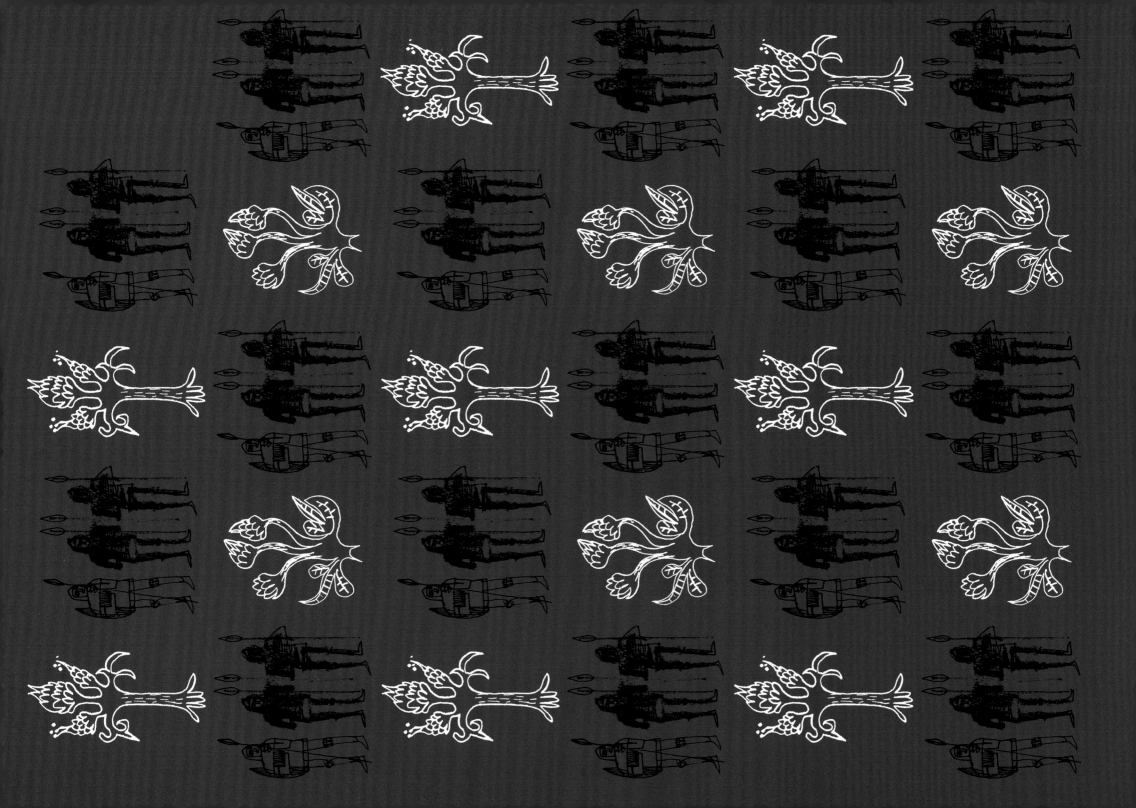

ROBERT THE BRUCE

KING OF SCOTS

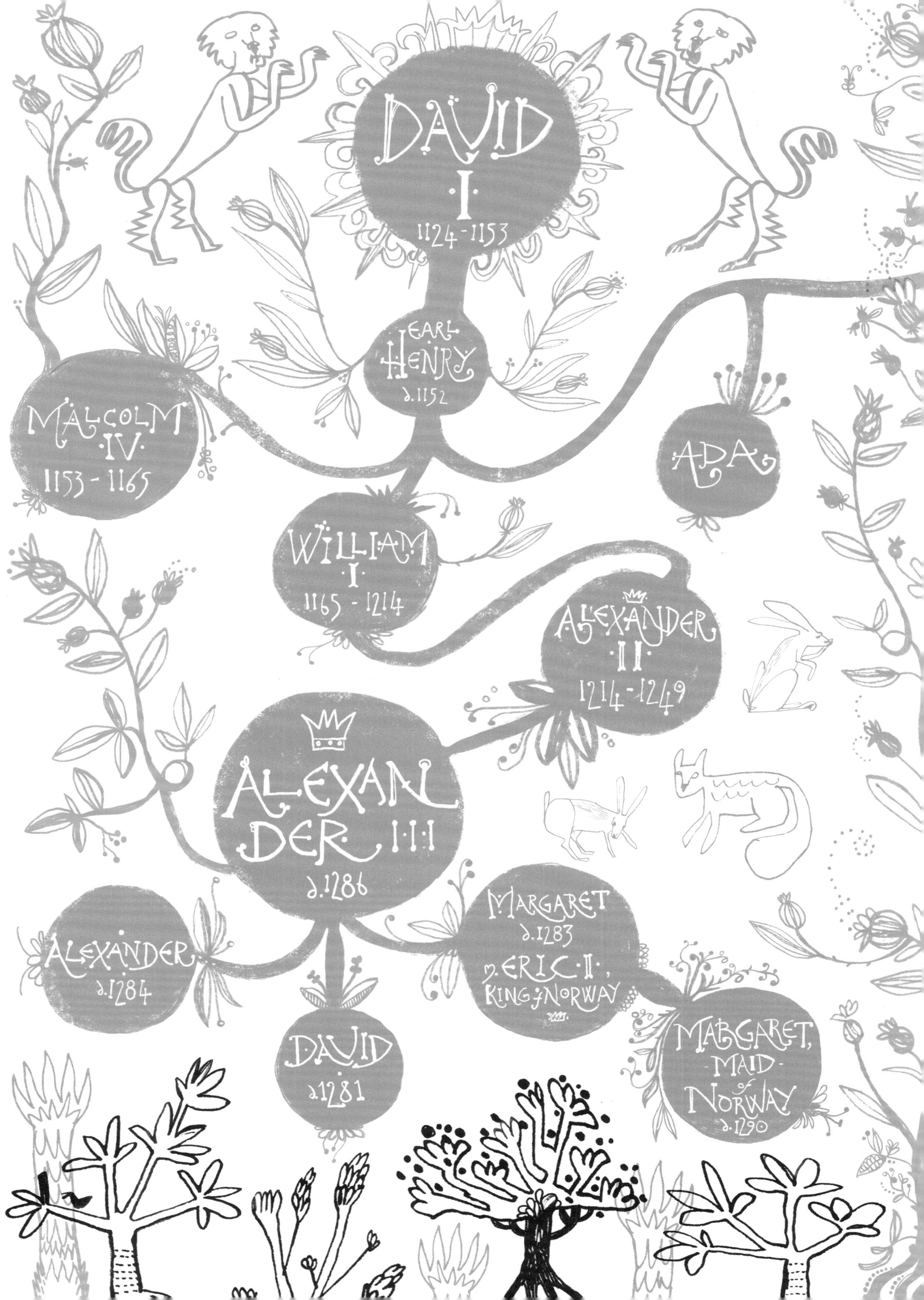
DAVID I 1124 - 1153
EARL HENRY d.1152
MALCOLM IV 1153 - 1165
ADA
WILLIAM I 1165 - 1214
ALEXANDER II 1214 - 1249
ALEXANDER III d.1286
ALEXANDER d.1284
DAVID d.1281
MARGARET d.1283 m. ERIC II, KING of NORWAY
MARGARET, MAID of NORWAY d.1290

ROBERT THE BRUCE

KING OF SCOTS

JAMES ROBERTSON

Illustrated by

JILL CALDER

BIRLINN
2014

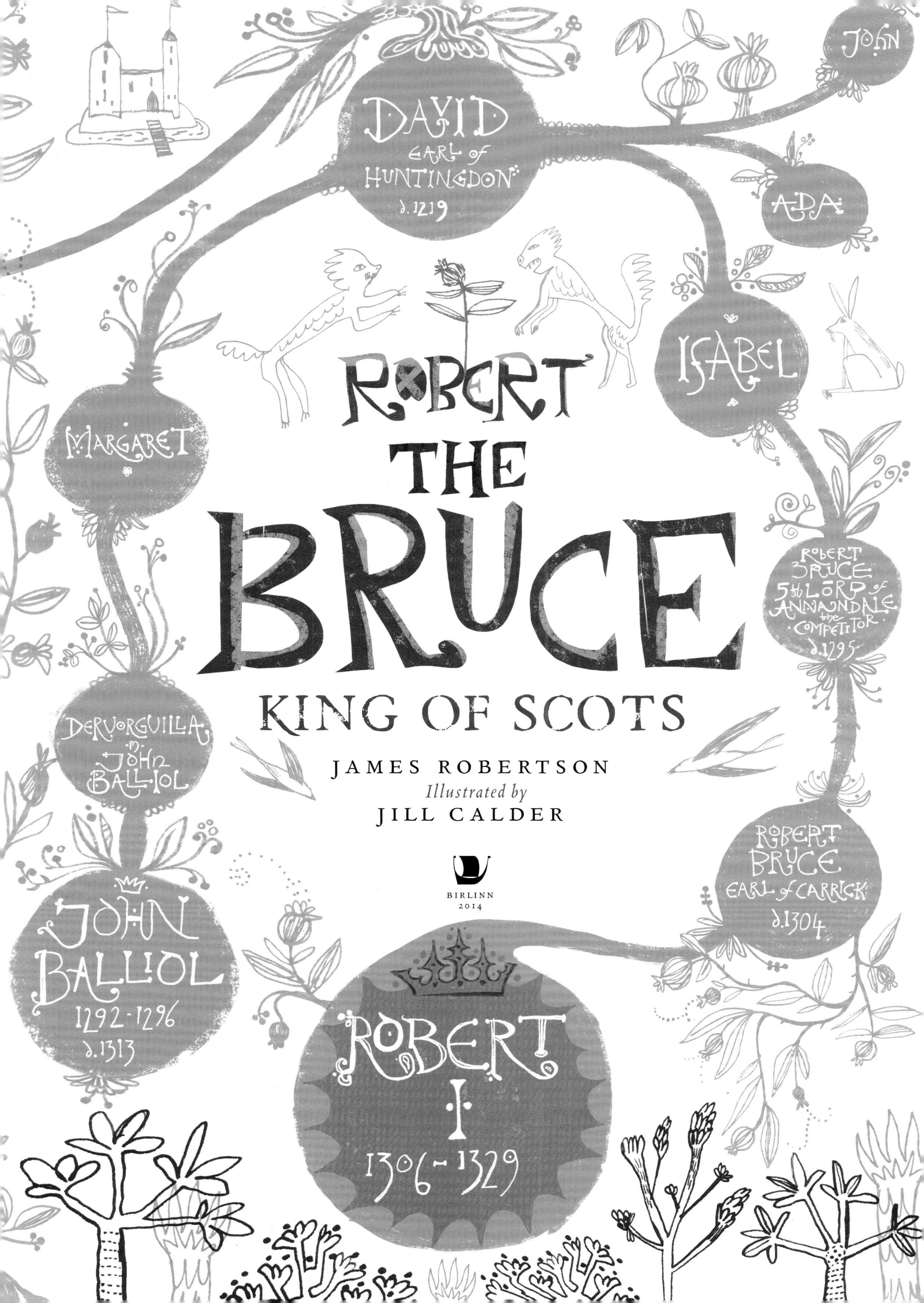
DAVID EARL of HUNTINGDON d.1219
JOHN
ADA
ISABEL
MARGARET
ROBERT BRUCE 5th LORD of ANNANDALE the COMPETITOR d.1295
DERVORGUILLA m. JOHN BALLIOL
ROBERT BRUCE EARL of CARRICK d.1304
JOHN BALLIOL 1292-1296 d.1313
ROBERT I 1306-1329

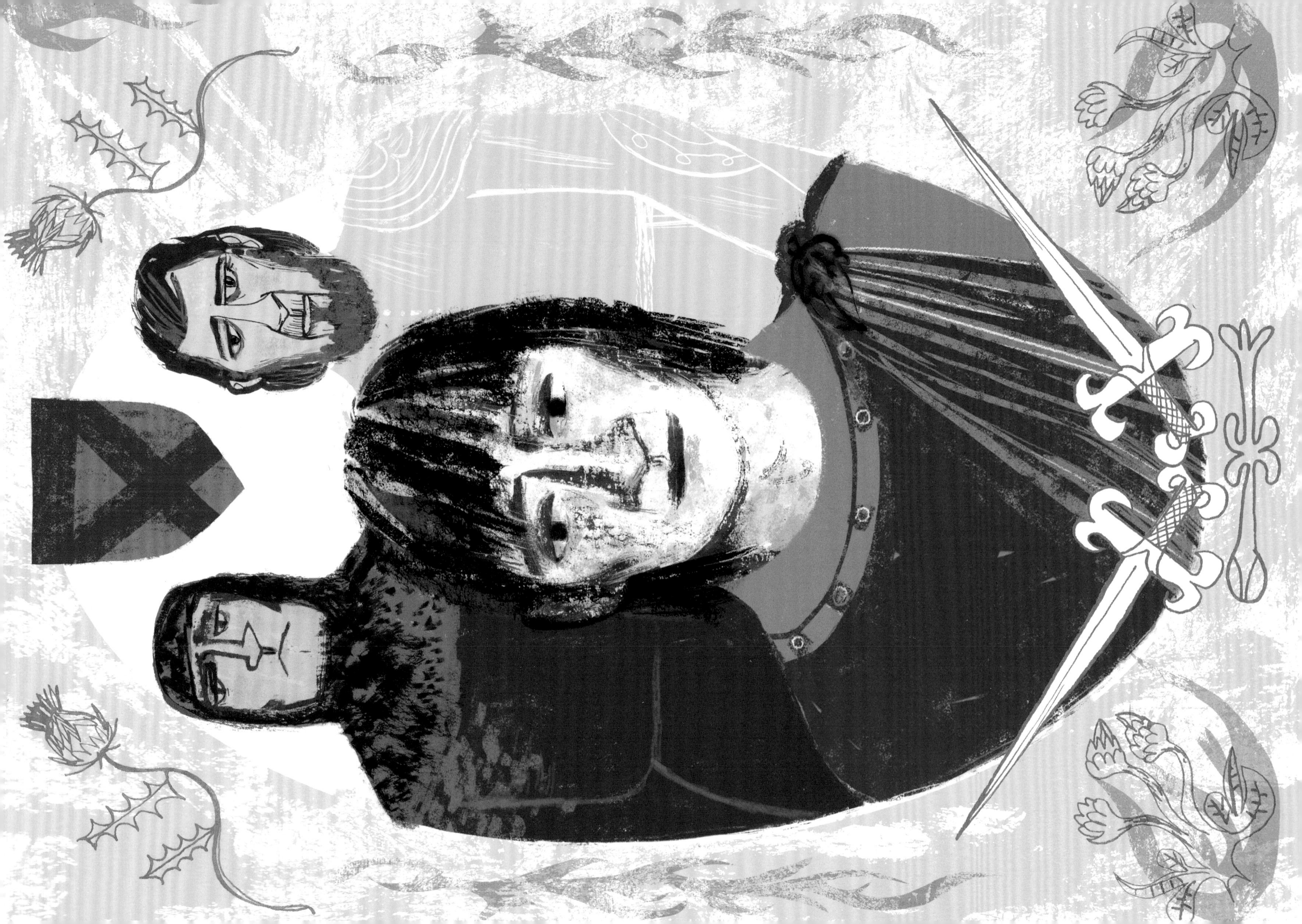

THIS IS THE STORY OF A MAN WHO BECAME A KING...

ROBERT BRUCE – or ROBERT I of SCOTLAND as he would become – was born in 1274. His birthplace is thought to have been Turnberry Castle in Ayrshire. His Norman ancestors, called de Brus, had come to England with William the Conqueror in 1066, and arrived in Scotland sixty years later. By the time of Robert's birth, the Bruces were one of the most powerful families in the land. But when he was only twelve an event took place which left the throne of Scotland empty and the country's future uncertain, and which would set the course for the rest of Bruce's life.

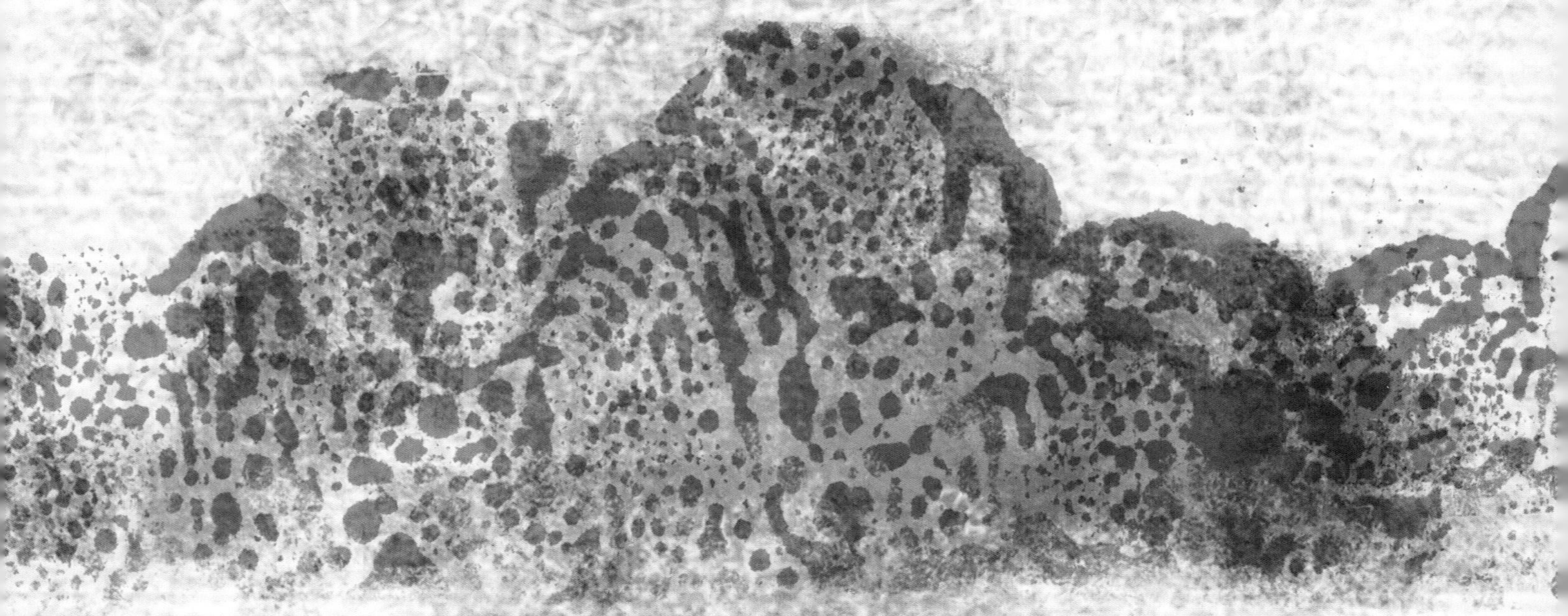

On a stormy afternoon in March 1286, Alexander III, King of Scots, set out from Edinburgh to the ferry point on the south side of the Firth of Forth. Defying the wild weather, he insisted on being rowed across the water to Inverkeithing in Fife. From there he rode along the coast to the royal manor at Kinghorn, to be with his new young French wife Yolande. But he never arrived. The next morning his body was found on the shore, where he had fallen from his horse and broken his neck.

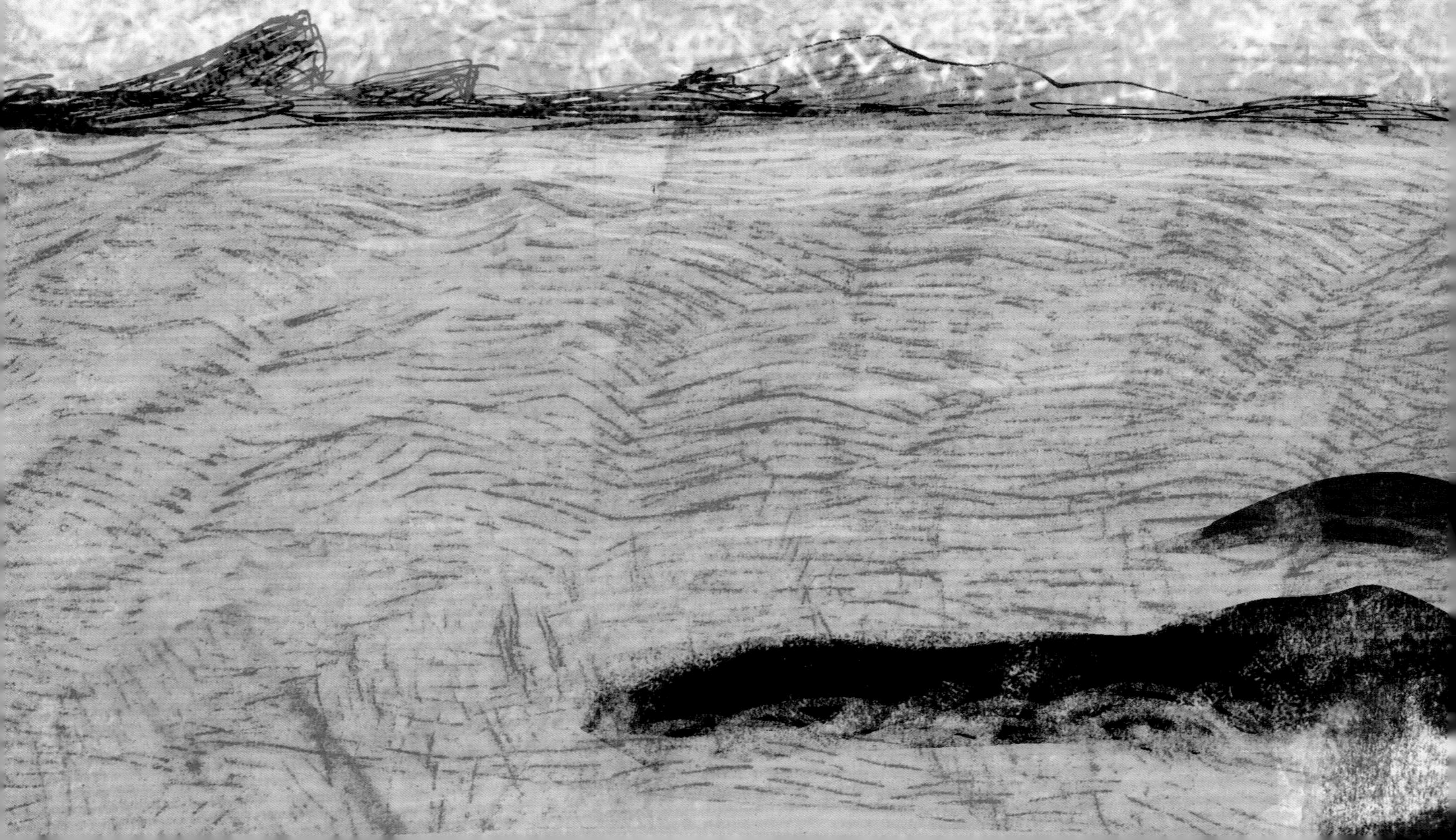

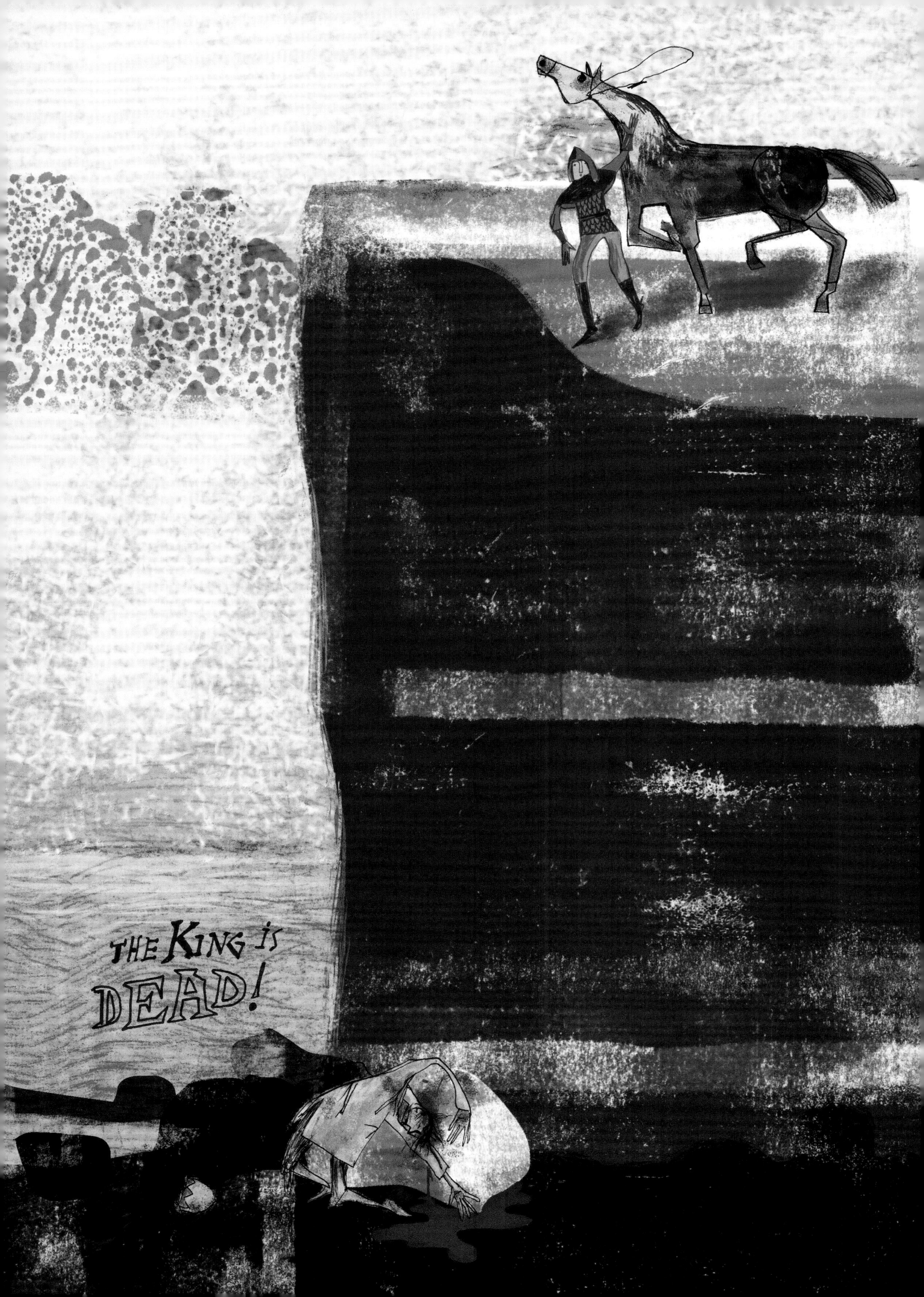
THE KING IS DEAD!

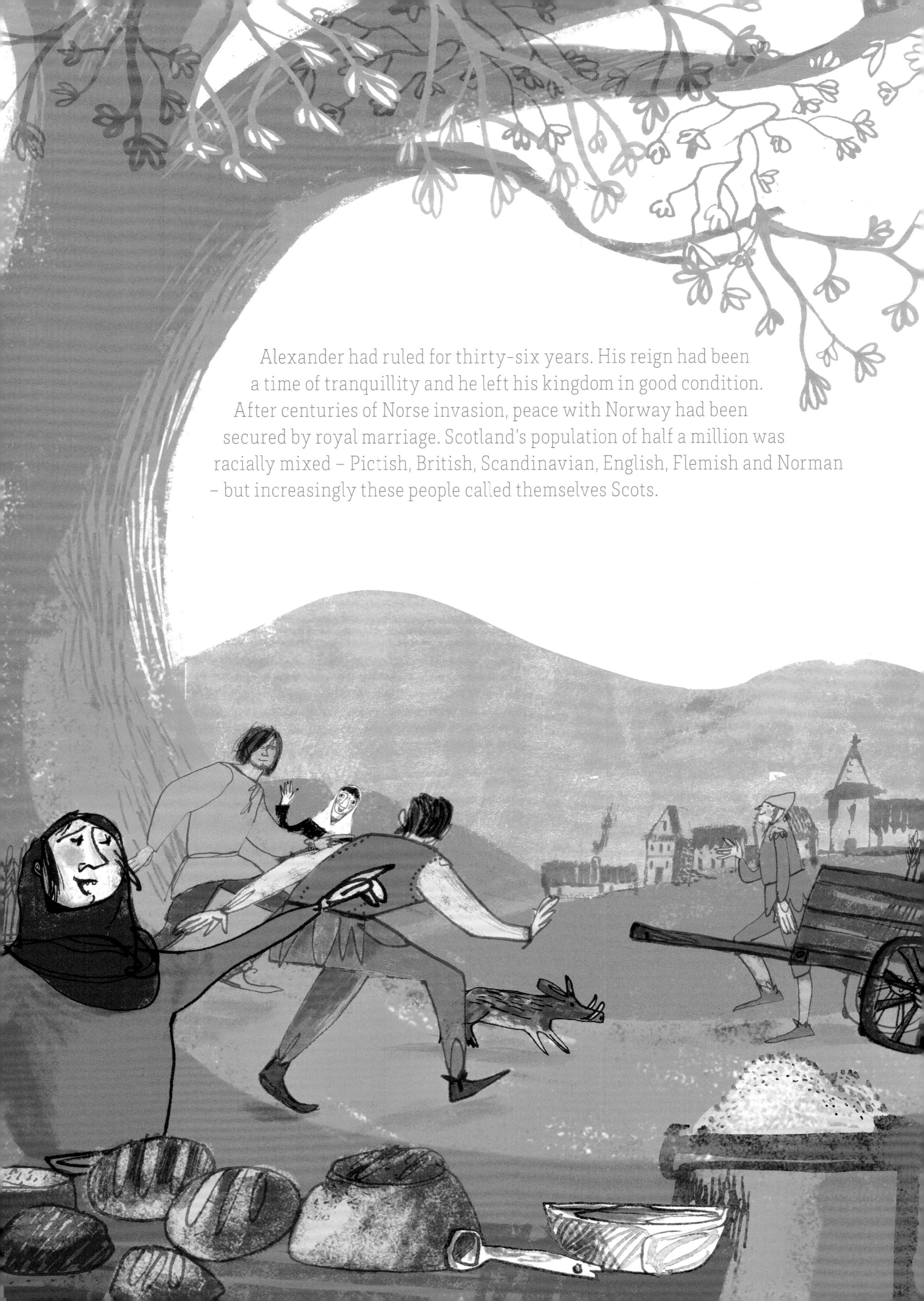

Alexander had ruled for thirty-six years. His reign had been a time of tranquillity and he left his kingdom in good condition. After centuries of Norse invasion, peace with Norway had been secured by royal marriage. Scotland's population of half a million was racially mixed – Pictish, British, Scandinavian, English, Flemish and Norman – but increasingly these people called themselves Scots.

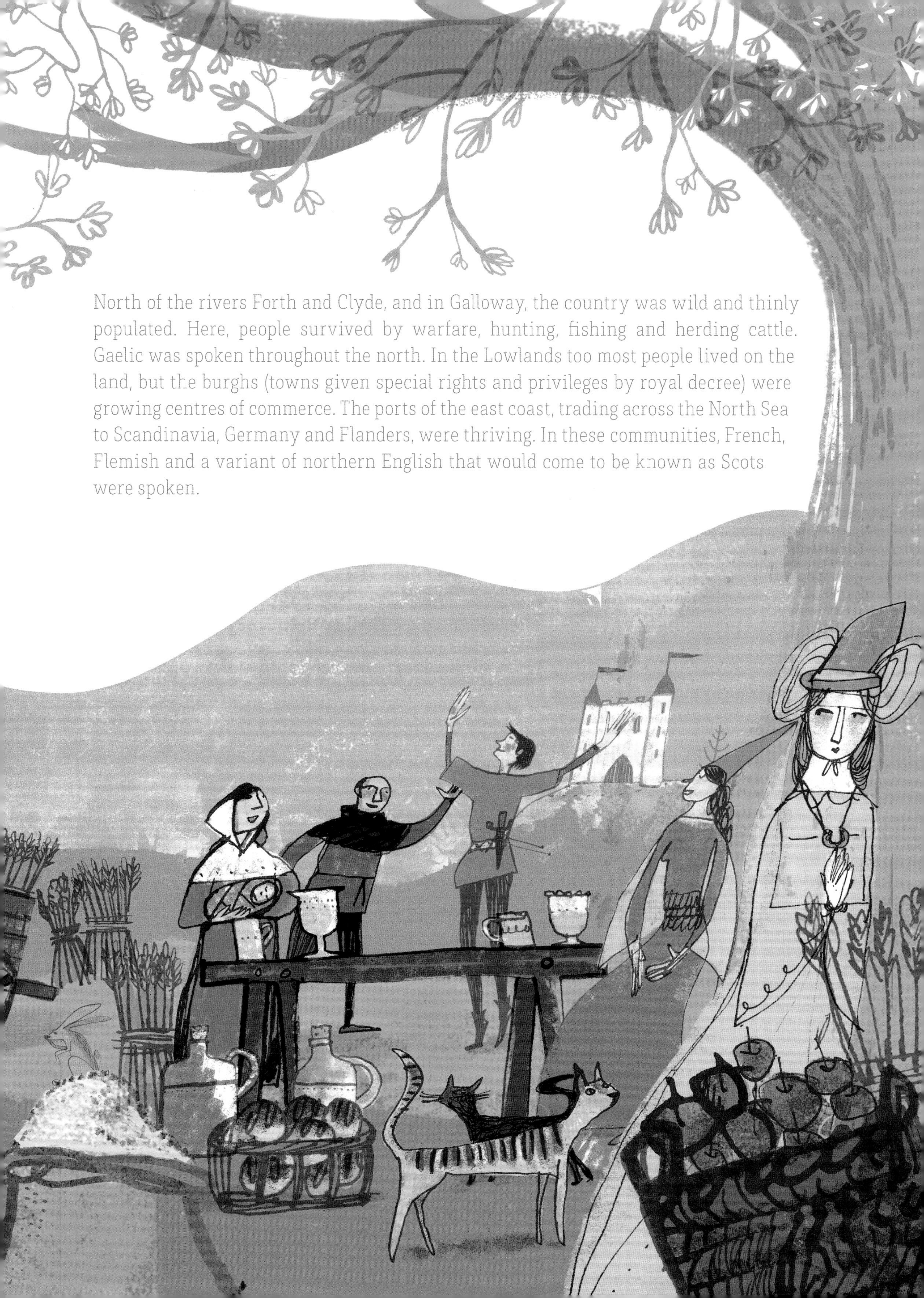

North of the rivers Forth and Clyde, and in Galloway, the country was wild and thinly populated. Here, people survived by warfare, hunting, fishing and herding cattle. Gaelic was spoken throughout the north. In the Lowlands too most people lived on the land, but the burghs (towns given special rights and privileges by royal decree) were growing centres of commerce. The ports of the east coast, trading across the North Sea to Scandinavia, Germany and Flanders, were thriving. In these communities, French, Flemish and a variant of northern English that would come to be known as Scots were spoken.

The royal household stayed mainly in the south of the country, moving between Stirling, Edinburgh, Roxburgh and other fortresses. The king was at the head of a feudal system of government, a model which the Normans had brought with them from Europe. Under this system, all men of rank owed allegiance or 'fealty' to their superior lord: in return for his protection and the right to use some of his land they gave him military service, rents and other dues. At the bottom of society were the peasants, who had no power but were bound to their immediate superiors by similar obligations.

From his first marriage Alexander had had two sons and a daughter, Margaret, who had become Queen of Norway. All three had died before him. The succession therefore rested with his infant granddaughter, also Margaret, but in 1290, as she was being brought across the sea from Norway, she became ill and died in Orkney.

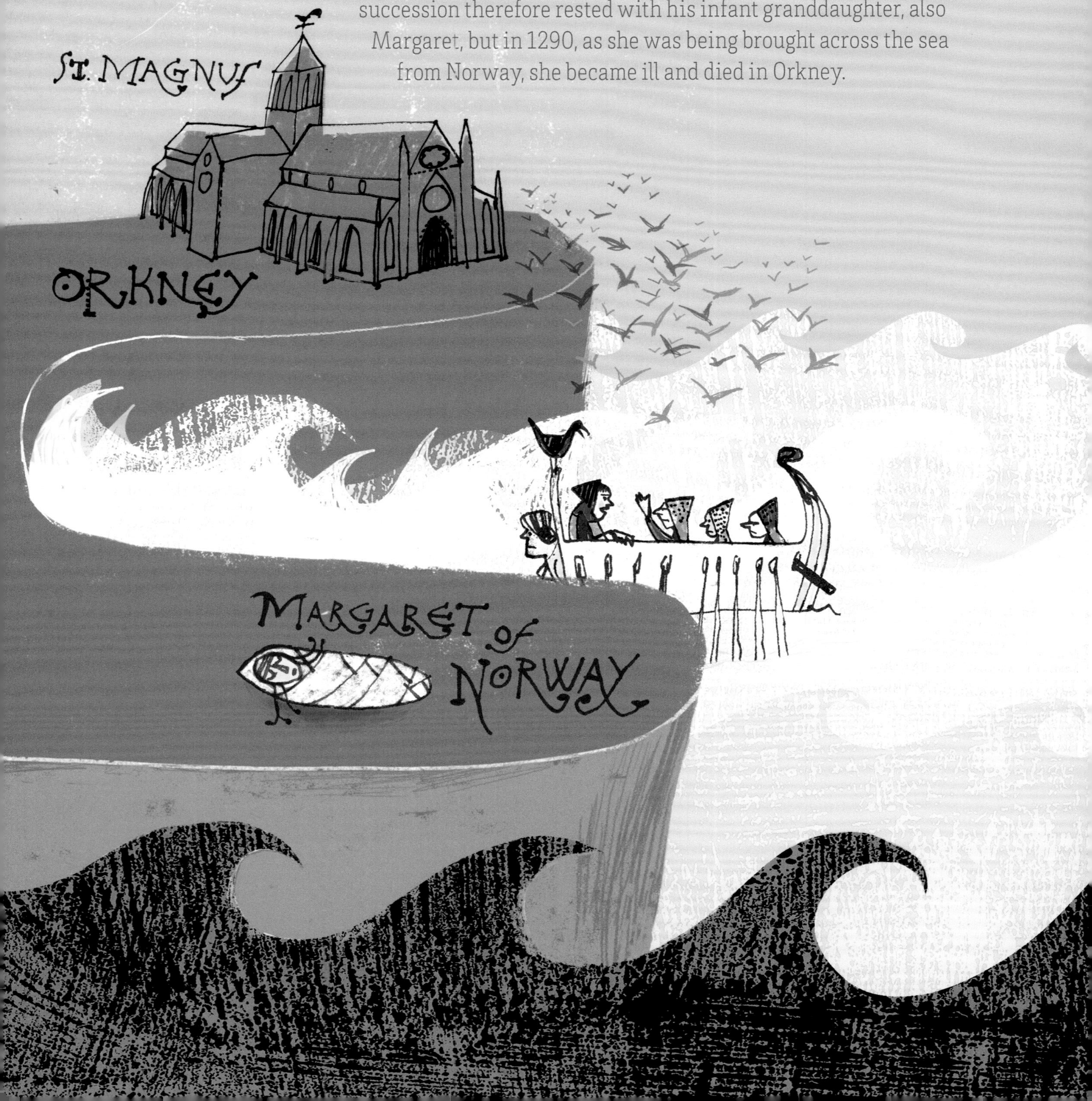
St. Magnus
Orkney
Margaret of Norway

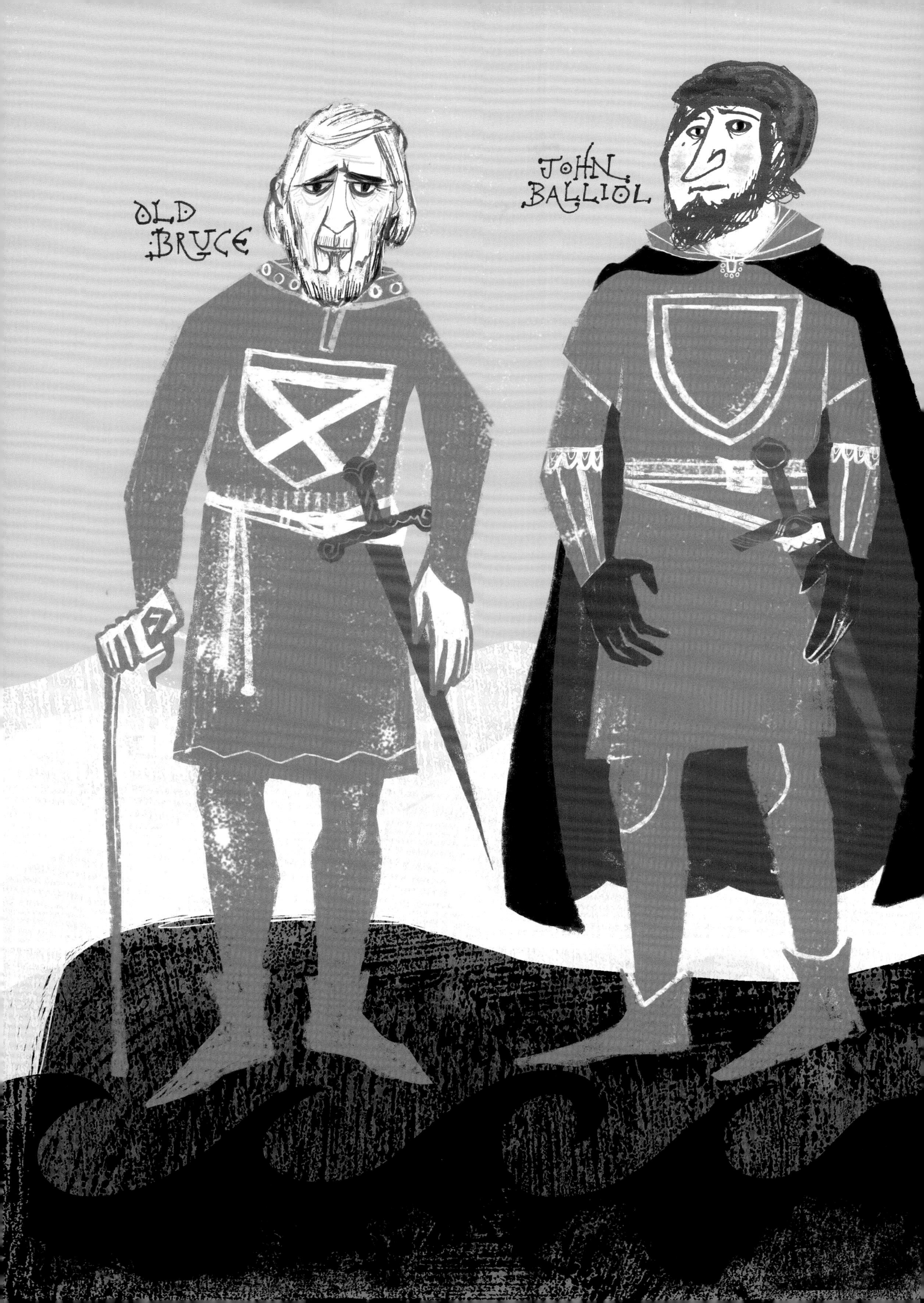
OLD BRUCE
JOHN BALLIOL

Since the King's death, guardians elected from among the earls, bishops and barons of Scotland had governed the country. Now they had to choose a new monarch. There were several claimants, but two men could trace their lineage directly back to David I, who had reigned more than 100 years before. One was the forty-year-old John Balliol, Lord of Galloway. The other was Robert Bruce, Earl of Carrick and Lord of Annandale, the grandfather of the Robert Bruce who is the subject of this book. Known as 'the Competitor', he was eighty, but still a man of great ambition. Both men had large estates in England as well as in Scotland.

To avoid the issue being settled by fighting, the Guardians called a council to hear the various claims. They asked Edward I, King of England – a larger and richer country than Scotland – to act as arbitrator.

In the summer of 1291 Edward invited the Scottish leaders to meet him at Norham Castle on the River Tweed, where he waited with a large army. When the Scots arrived, he announced that he had come not as a neutral umpire but as their feudal superior. 'Prove that I am *not* your overlord,' he challenged them.

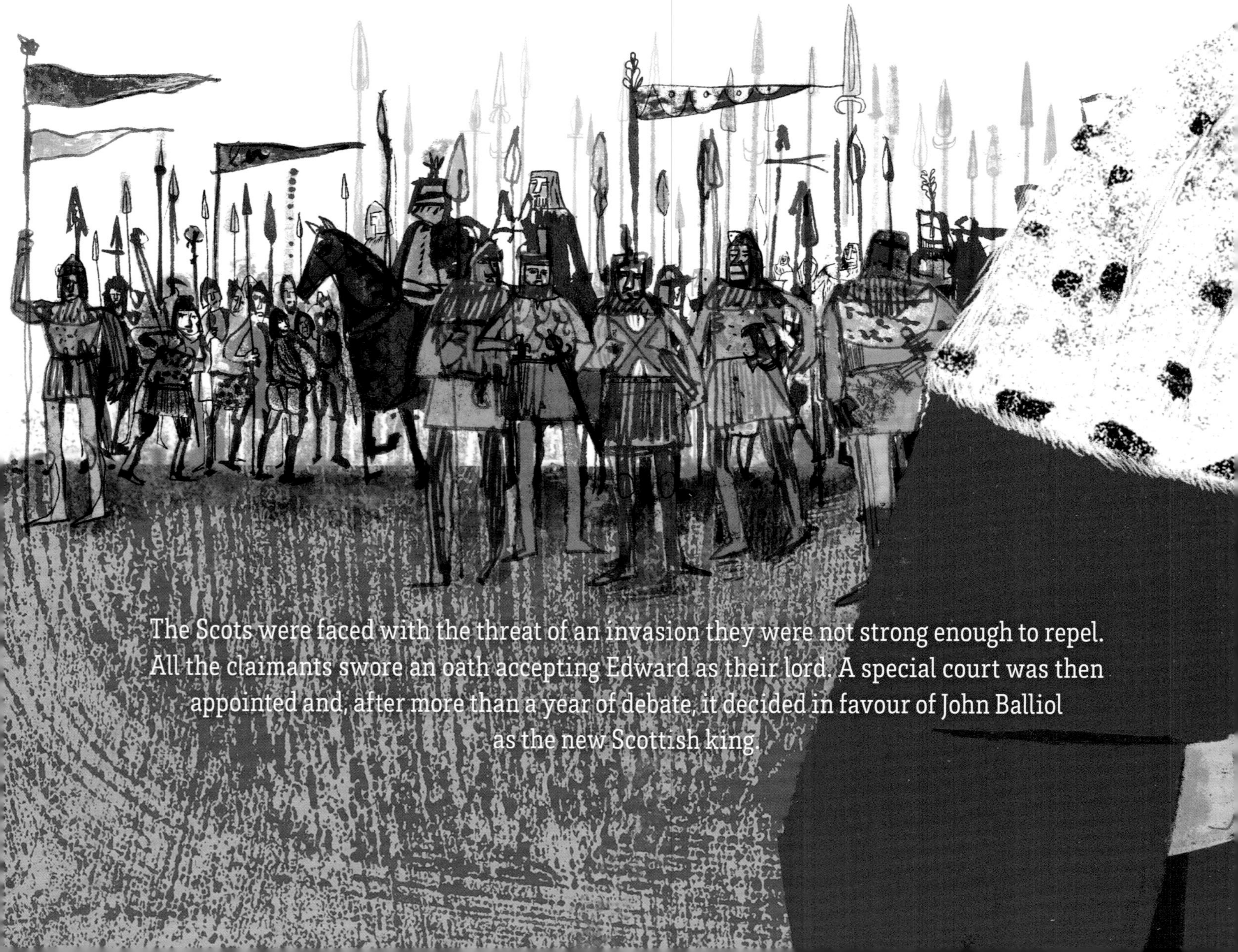

The Scots were faced with the threat of an invasion they were not strong enough to repel. All the claimants swore an oath accepting Edward as their lord. A special court was then appointed and, after more than a year of debate, it decided in favour of John Balliol as the new Scottish king.

Edward immediately demanded acts of homage and vows of fealty from Balliol. He wanted to show that the Scots must defer to the English Crown.

This was part of his plan to control all of the island of Britain so that he could concentrate his attention on gaining territory and power in France. Over the next few years, he conquered Wales, and further humiliated King John of Scotland by summoning him before the English Parliament and overturning his decisions. He also demanded Scottish military and financial support for his wars in France.

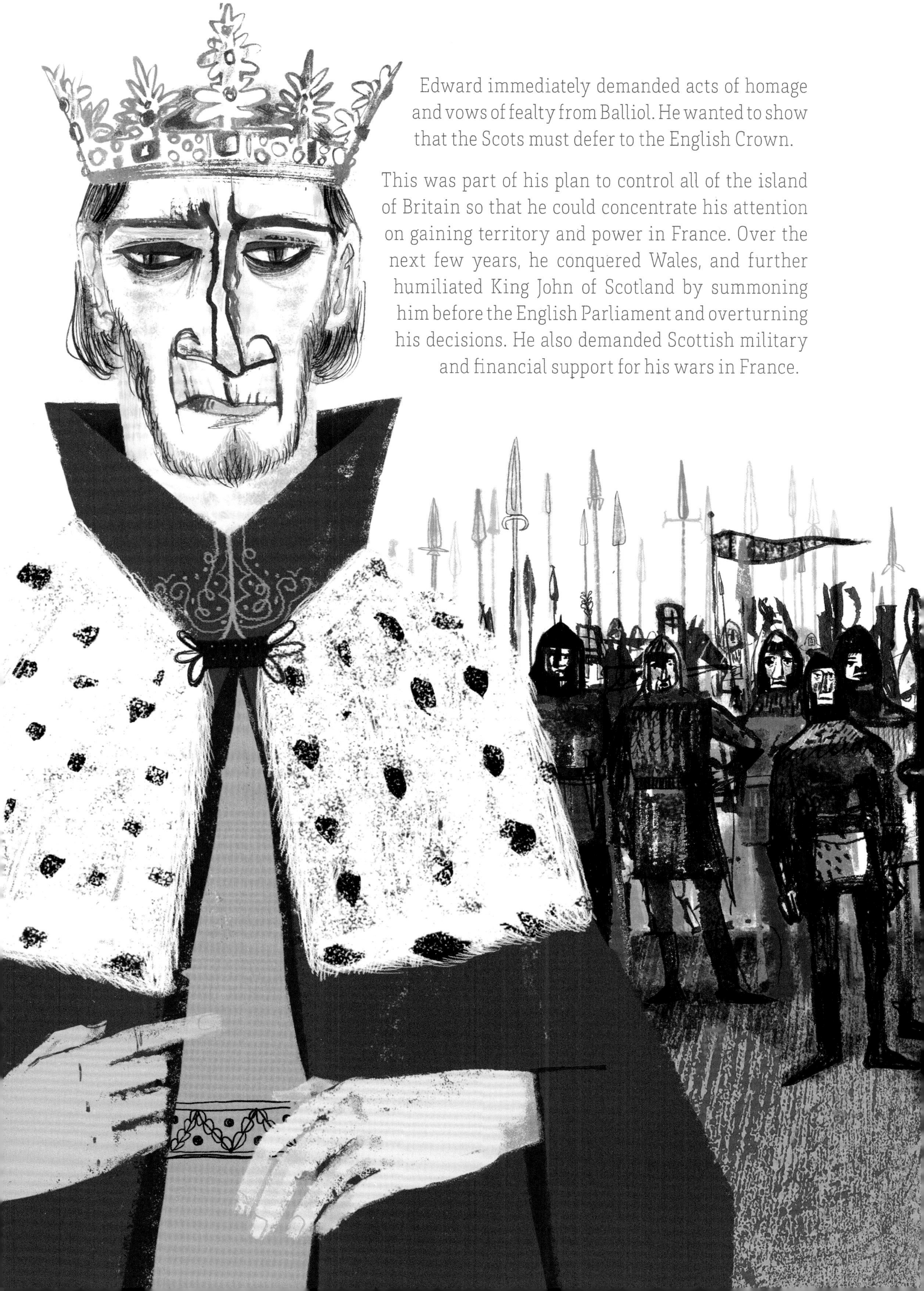

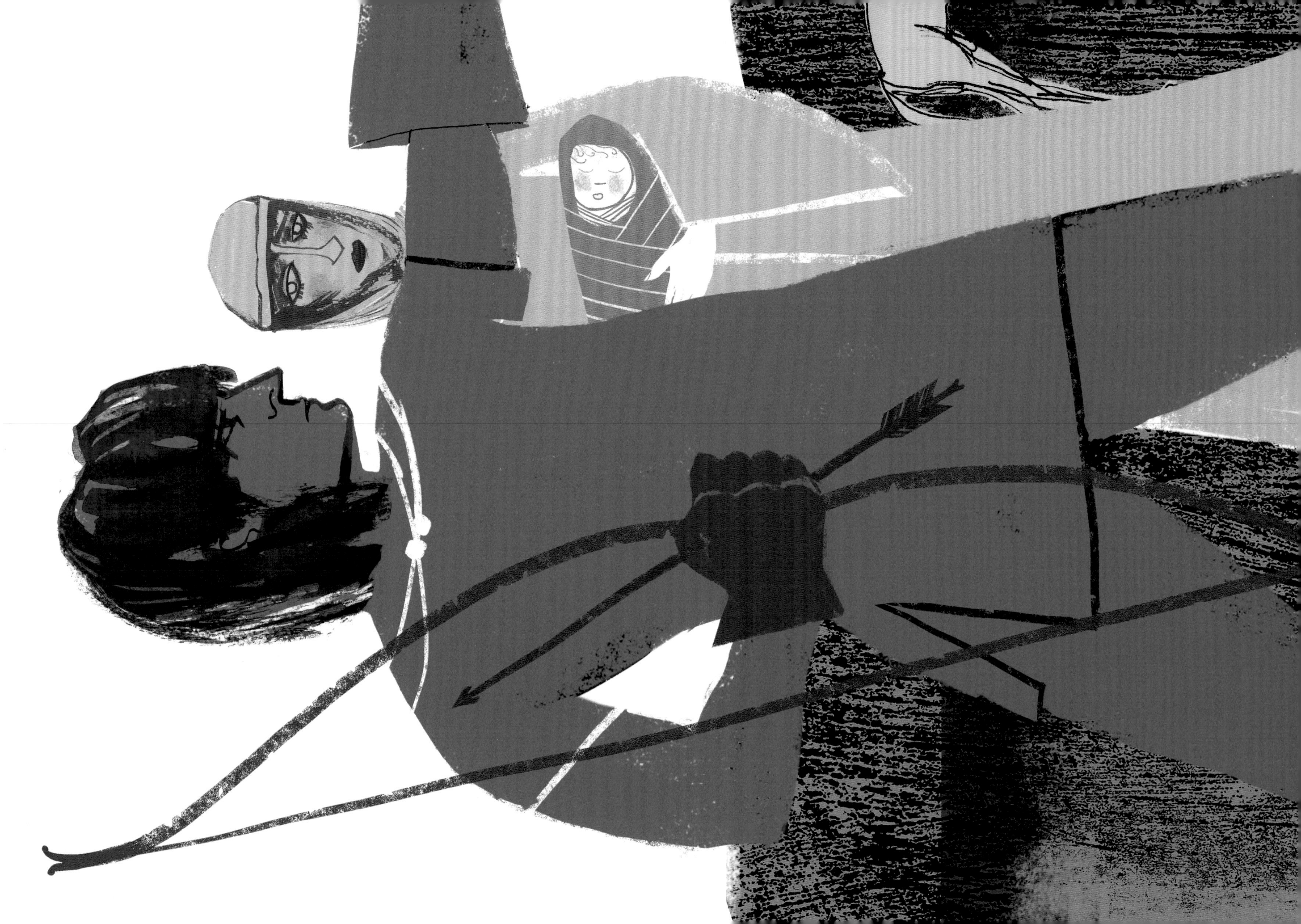

By 1296 the leading men of Scotland had had enough. They formed a new Council of Guardianship, taking power out of King John's hands, and negotiated a treaty of mutual defence with the French. Edward I's response was to prepare to invade Scotland. In the name of King John, the Scottish Council issued a call to all free men to gather under arms to repel the invader.

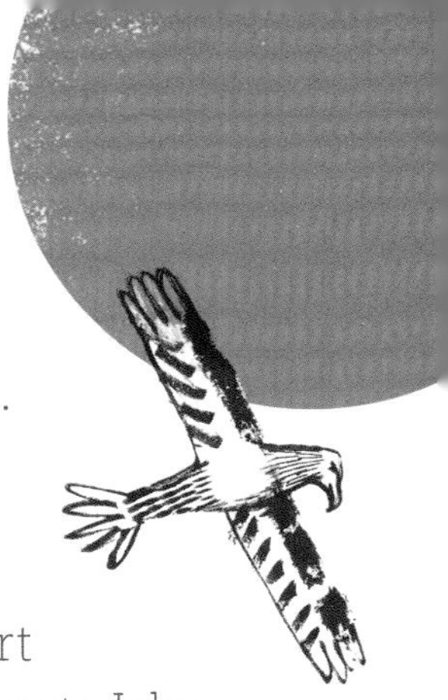

After losing their claim to the throne five years before, the Bruces had played little part in Scottish affairs. Bruce the Competitor had since died. His son, to avoid doing homage to John Balliol, had gone on an extended visit to Norway, only returning on his father's death. He had passed the earldom of Carrick to his son, the 22-year-old Robert, who had been spending time on the family's estates in the south of England and at Edward's court. Young Robert had also married Isabella, daughter of the Earl of Mar, but after giving birth to a daughter, Marjorie, Isabella died in 1296. It was no surprise when the Bruces, along with several other Scottish nobles, ignored the call to support King John. As a consequence, they forfeited the title to their lands, which were given to John Comyn, Earl of Buchan. The Comyns, another immensely powerful family, were closely allied to John Balliol.

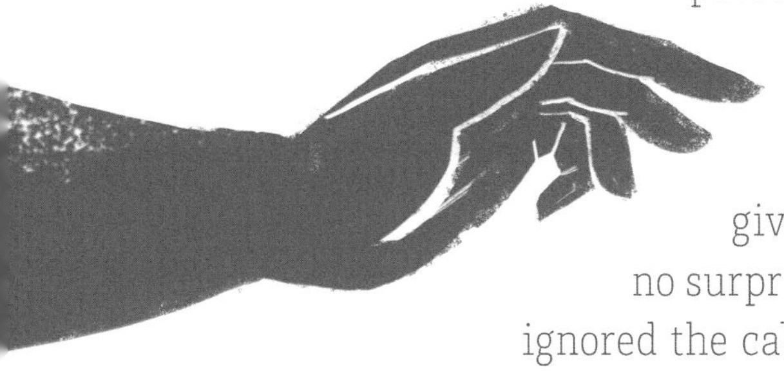

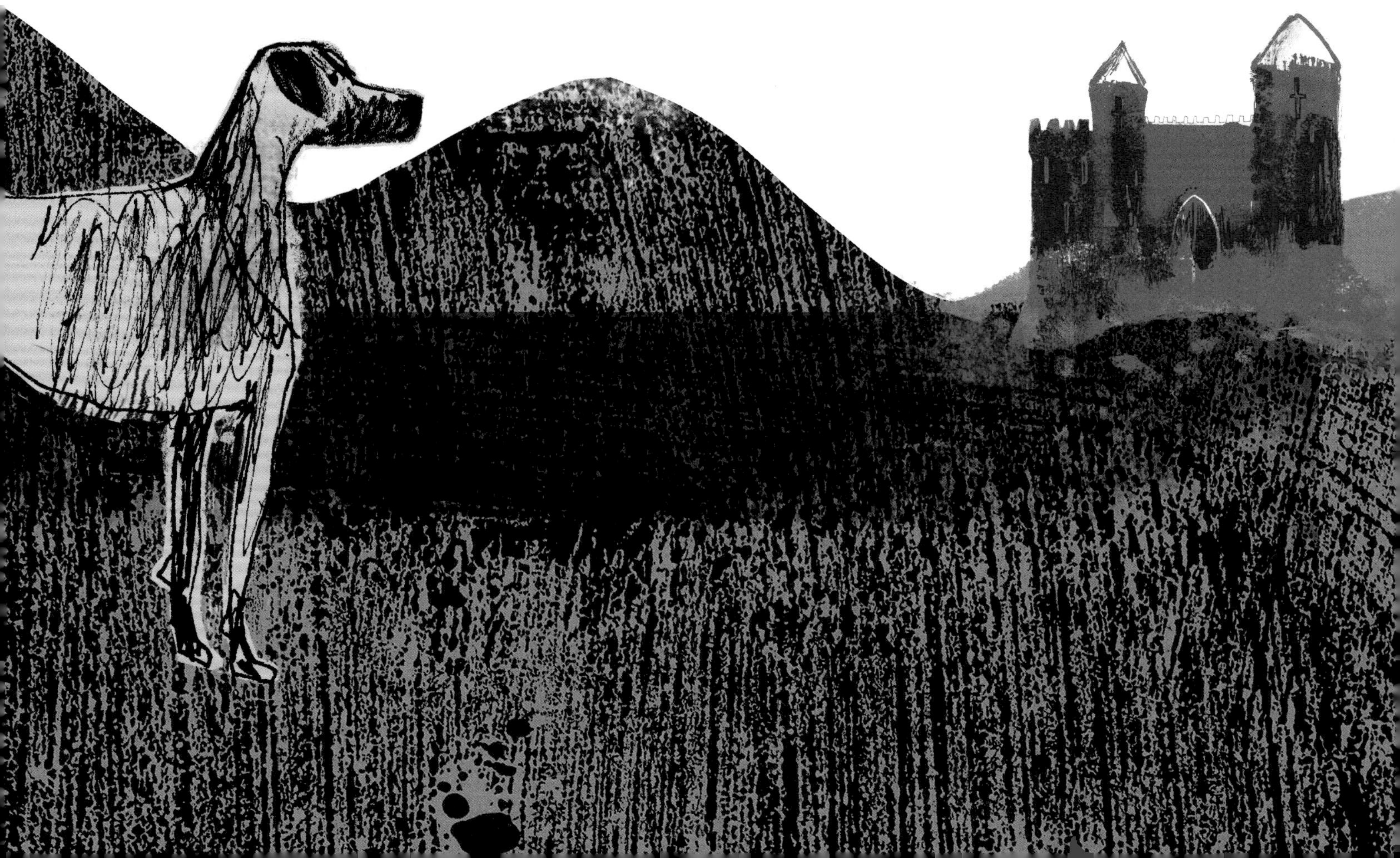

Edward invaded, seizing every important Scottish castle and killing or imprisoning any of the nobility who opposed him. Those who did not, including the Bruces, had no choice but to declare their loyalty to Edward. John Balliol was brought before Edward and forced to resign his kingdom and abdicate. The blazon of royalty was torn from his tabard, earning him the nickname 'Toom Tabard' ('Empty Shirt'). He was sent to England and held there under house arrest. When Robert Bruce, young Robert's father, suggested that he be allowed to take the throne in Balliol's place, Edward's reply was scathing: 'Have we nothing else to do but win kingdoms for you?'

English soldiers and administrators were brought north to fill every position of authority and control. Edward ordered the removal of the Scottish regalia to London, and the Stone of Destiny, on which generations of Scottish kings had been enthroned, was sent from Scone, near Perth, to Westminster Abbey. The subjugation of Scotland seemed complete.

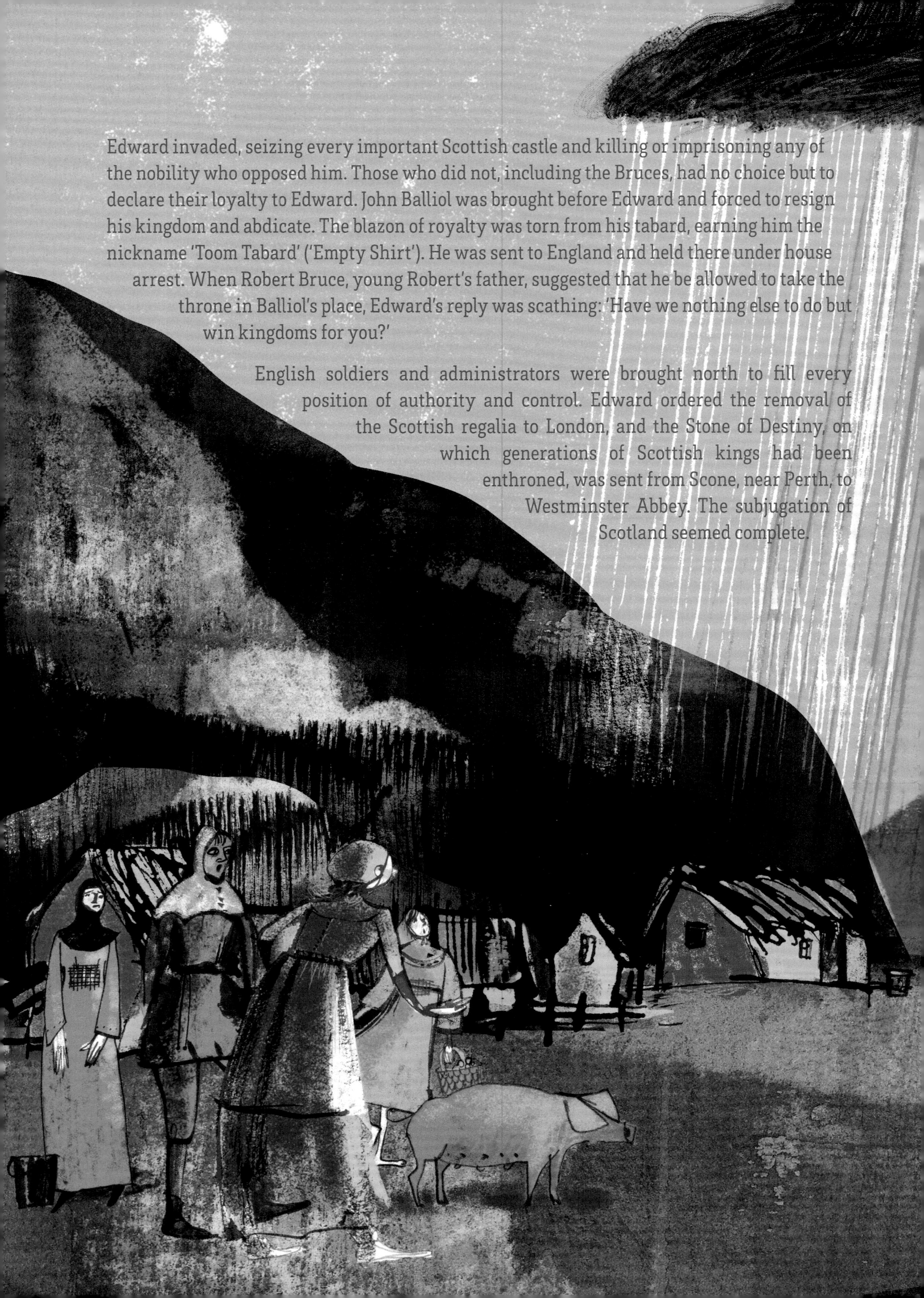

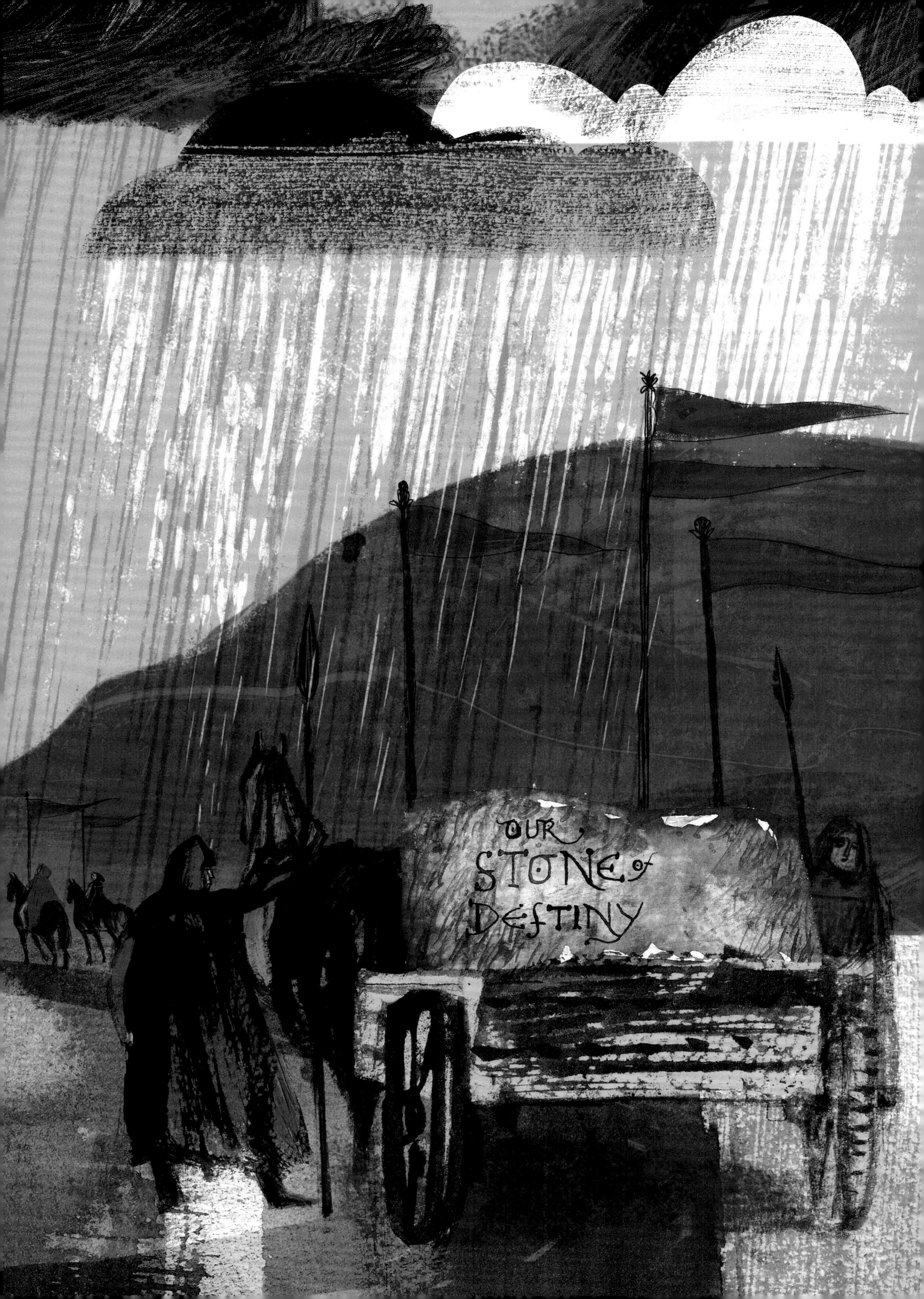
OUR STONE of DESTINY

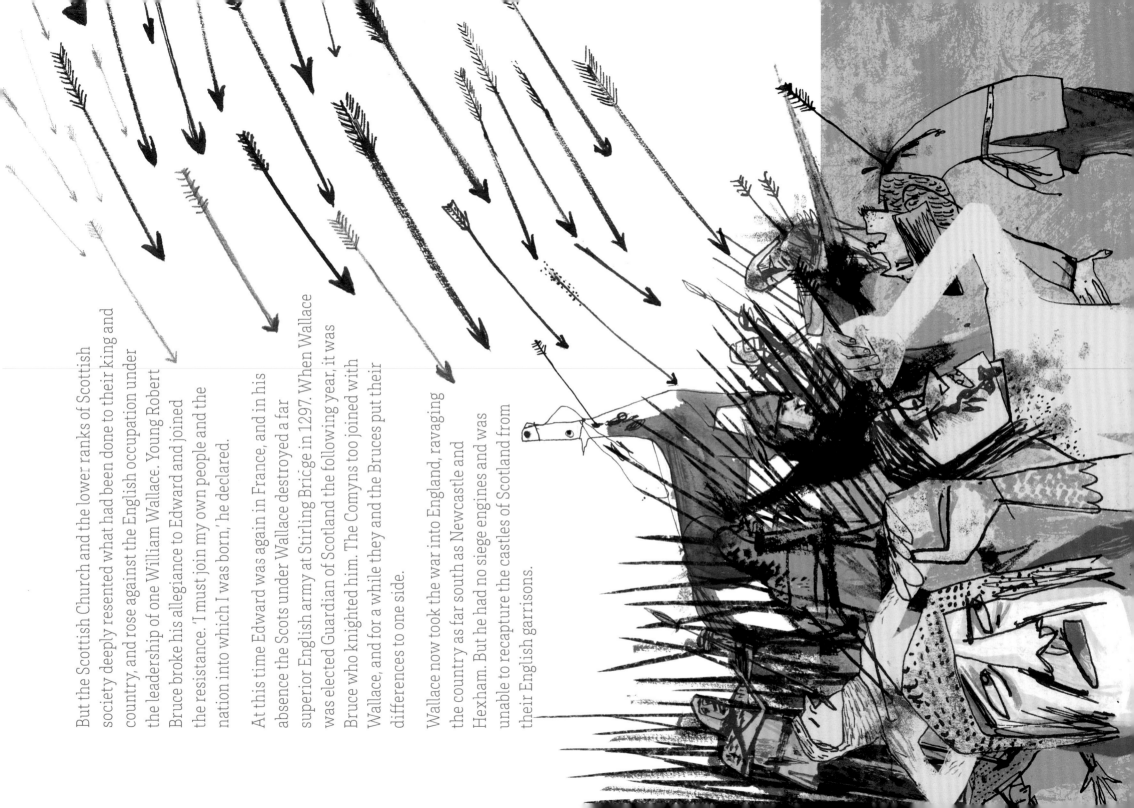

But the Scottish Church and the lower ranks of Scottish society deeply resented what had been done to their king and country, and rose against the English occupation under the leadership of one William Wallace. Young Robert Bruce broke his allegiance to Edward and joined the resistance. 'I must join my own people and the nation into which I was born,' he declared.

At this time Edward was again in France, and in his absence the Scots under Wallace destroyed a far superior English army at Stirling Bridge in 1297. When Wallace was elected Guardian of Scotland the following year, it was Bruce who knighted him. The Comyns too joined with Wallace, and for a while they and the Bruces put their differences to one side.

Wallace now took the war into England, ravaging the country as far south as Newcastle and Hexham. But he had no siege engines and was unable to recapture the castles of Scotland from their English garrisons.

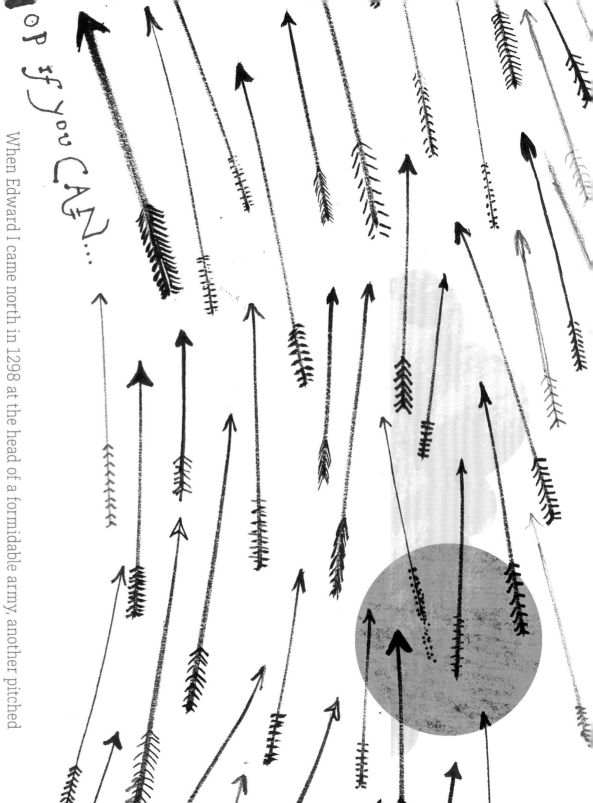

op if you can...

When Edward I came north in 1298 at the head of a formidable army, another pitched battle took place at Falkirk. 'I have brought you to the ring; hop if you can,' was Wallace's ironic incitement to his troops.

The Scots formed themselves into 'schiltrons' or hedgehog-like packs of spearmen, intended to withstand the assaults of the English heavy cavalry and protect their archers who stood behind them. But the English knights outflanked the Scots and concentrated their attack first on the inferior Scottish cavalry, who broke and fled the field, then on the archers, whom they killed in large numbers. The Scottish spearmen were thus left exposed to the relentless arrows of the English archers and crossbowmen, and the schiltrons were broken apart. Great slaughter ensued, and Wallace only narrowly escaped.

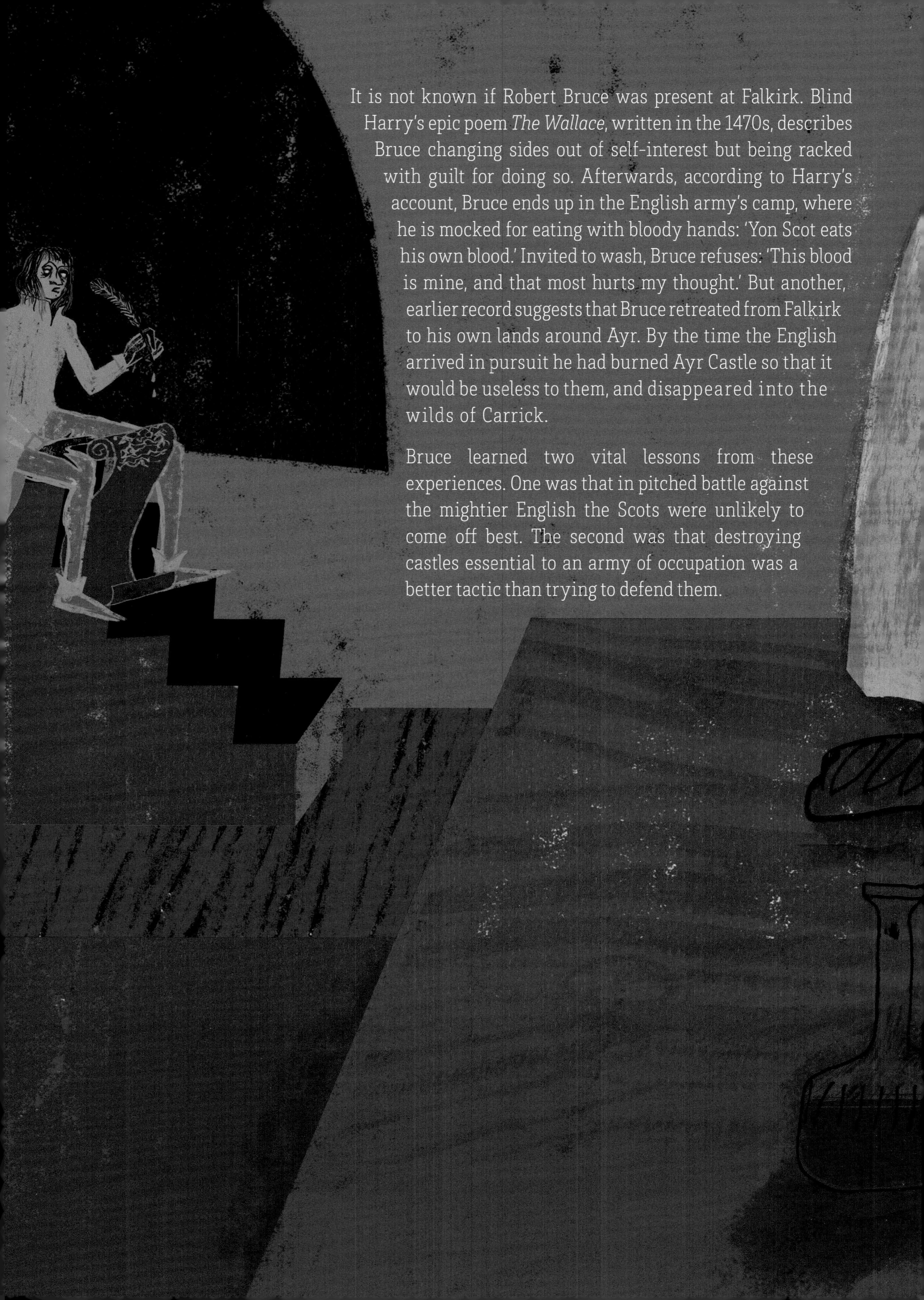

It is not known if Robert Bruce was present at Falkirk. Blind Harry's epic poem *The Wallace*, written in the 1470s, describes Bruce changing sides out of self-interest but being racked with guilt for doing so. Afterwards, according to Harry's account, Bruce ends up in the English army's camp, where he is mocked for eating with bloody hands: 'Yon Scot eats his own blood.' Invited to wash, Bruce refuses: 'This blood is mine, and that most hurts my thought.' But another, earlier record suggests that Bruce retreated from Falkirk to his own lands around Ayr. By the time the English arrived in pursuit he had burned Ayr Castle so that it would be useless to them, and disappeared into the wilds of Carrick.

Bruce learned two vital lessons from these experiences. One was that in pitched battle against the mightier English the Scots were unlikely to come off best. The second was that destroying castles essential to an army of occupation was a better tactic than trying to defend them.

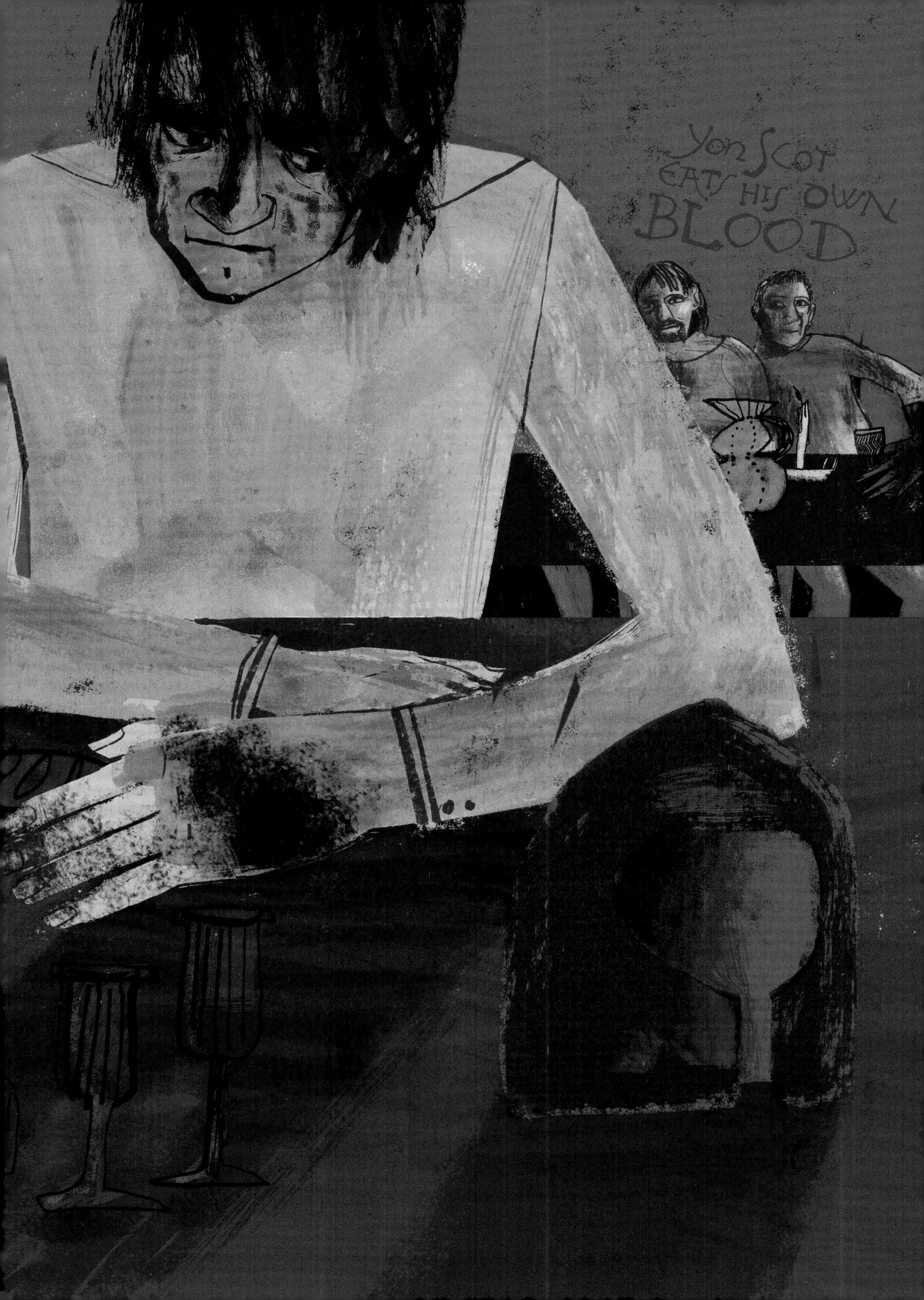
Yon Scot
eats his own
BLOOD

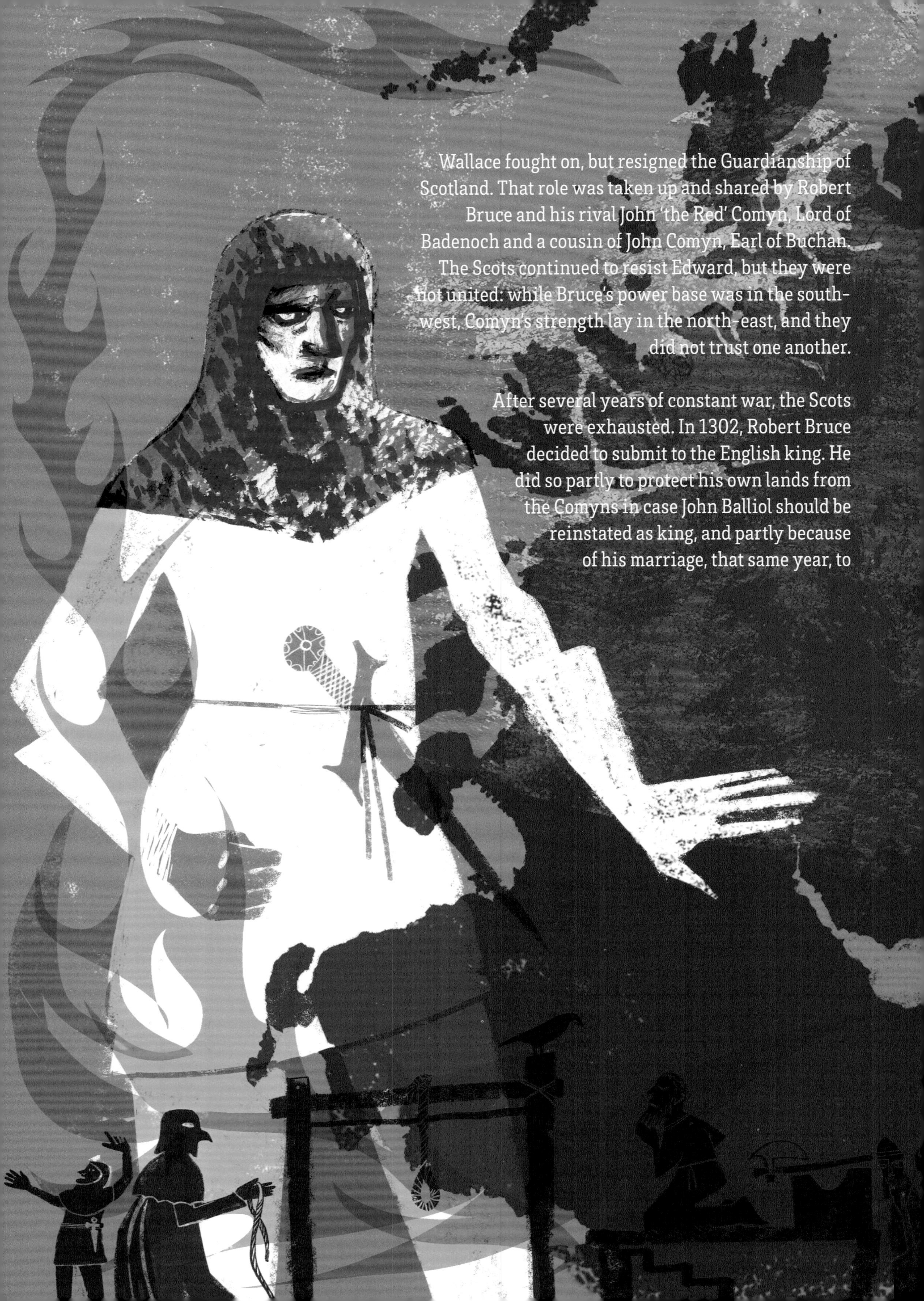

Wallace fought on, but resigned the Guardianship of Scotland. That role was taken up and shared by Robert Bruce and his rival John 'the Red' Comyn, Lord of Badenoch and a cousin of John Comyn, Earl of Buchan. The Scots continued to resist Edward, but they were not united: while Bruce's power base was in the south-west, Comyn's strength lay in the north-east, and they did not trust one another.

After several years of constant war, the Scots were exhausted. In 1302, Robert Bruce decided to submit to the English king. He did so partly to protect his own lands from the Comyns in case John Balliol should be reinstated as king, and partly because of his marriage, that same year, to

Elizabeth de Burgh, daughter of the Earl of Ulster, one of Edward's staunchest allies. The next year, with Bruce neutralised, Edward launched a ferocious assault, laying waste to towns and countryside across Scotland. The Red Comyn and his allies were forced to surrender and swear allegiance to the English king. Finally, it appeared, Scotland was under Edward's total control.

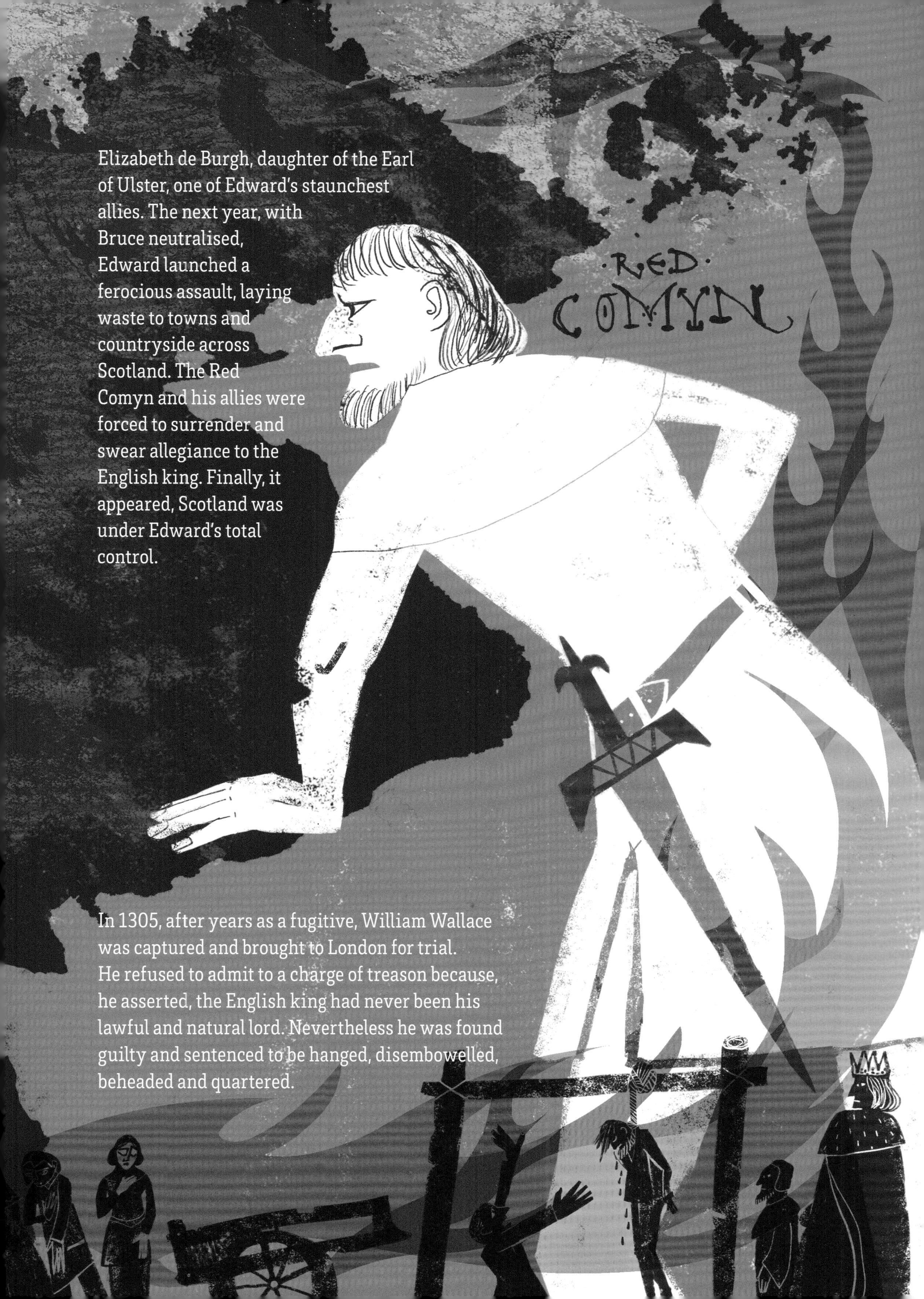
RED
COMYN

In 1305, after years as a fugitive, William Wallace was captured and brought to London for trial. He refused to admit to a charge of treason because, he asserted, the English king had never been his lawful and natural lord. Nevertheless he was found guilty and sentenced to be hanged, disembowelled, beheaded and quartered.

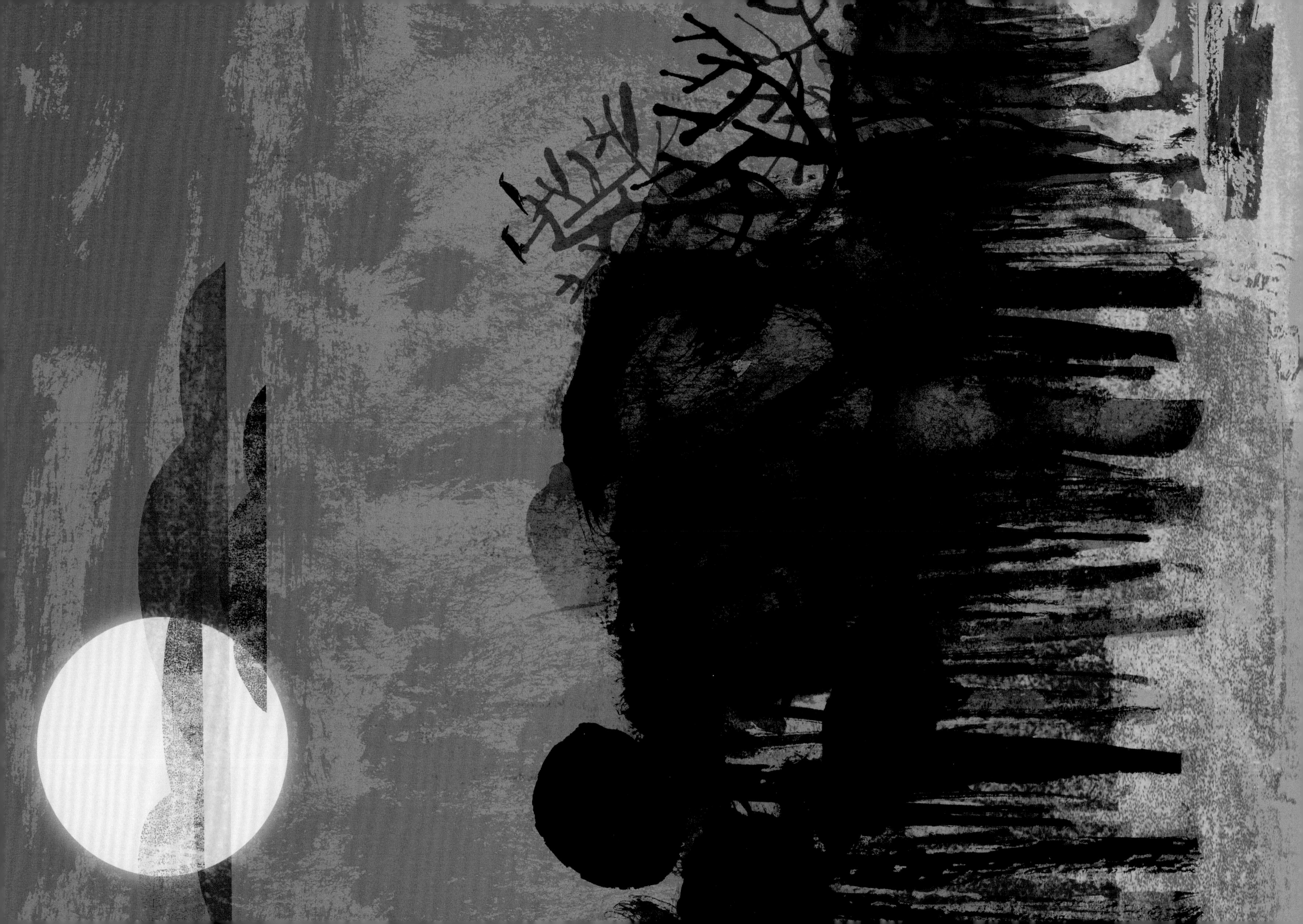

The judicial butchering of the heroic Wallace enraged and appalled the Scots, including both Bruce and Comyn. One story has it that they signed a pact: if Comyn backed Bruce in a fresh bid for the Scottish crown, Bruce, in return, would hand over all his lands to Comyn. However, Comyn promptly told Edward of the plot. Bruce was at the English court at this time. While at his lodgings, a friend sent a messenger with twelve pence and a pair of spurs. Taking the hint that he should immediately escape to Scotland, Bruce tipped the messenger with the money, put on the spurs and rode at great speed to his castle at Lochmaben.

Comyn was at Dumfries, and Bruce confronted him at the Greyfriars' church there on a cold February day in 1306. Left alone by their followers, they broke into an argument, and Bruce stabbed Comyn before the high altar. Bruce rushed from the church, whereupon his friend Roger Fitzpatrick asked what had happened. 'I doubt I have killed the Red Comyn,' said Bruce. 'Do you doubt?' Fitzpatrick replied. 'Then I'll mak siccar [make certain],' and he went inside to finish off the wounded man.

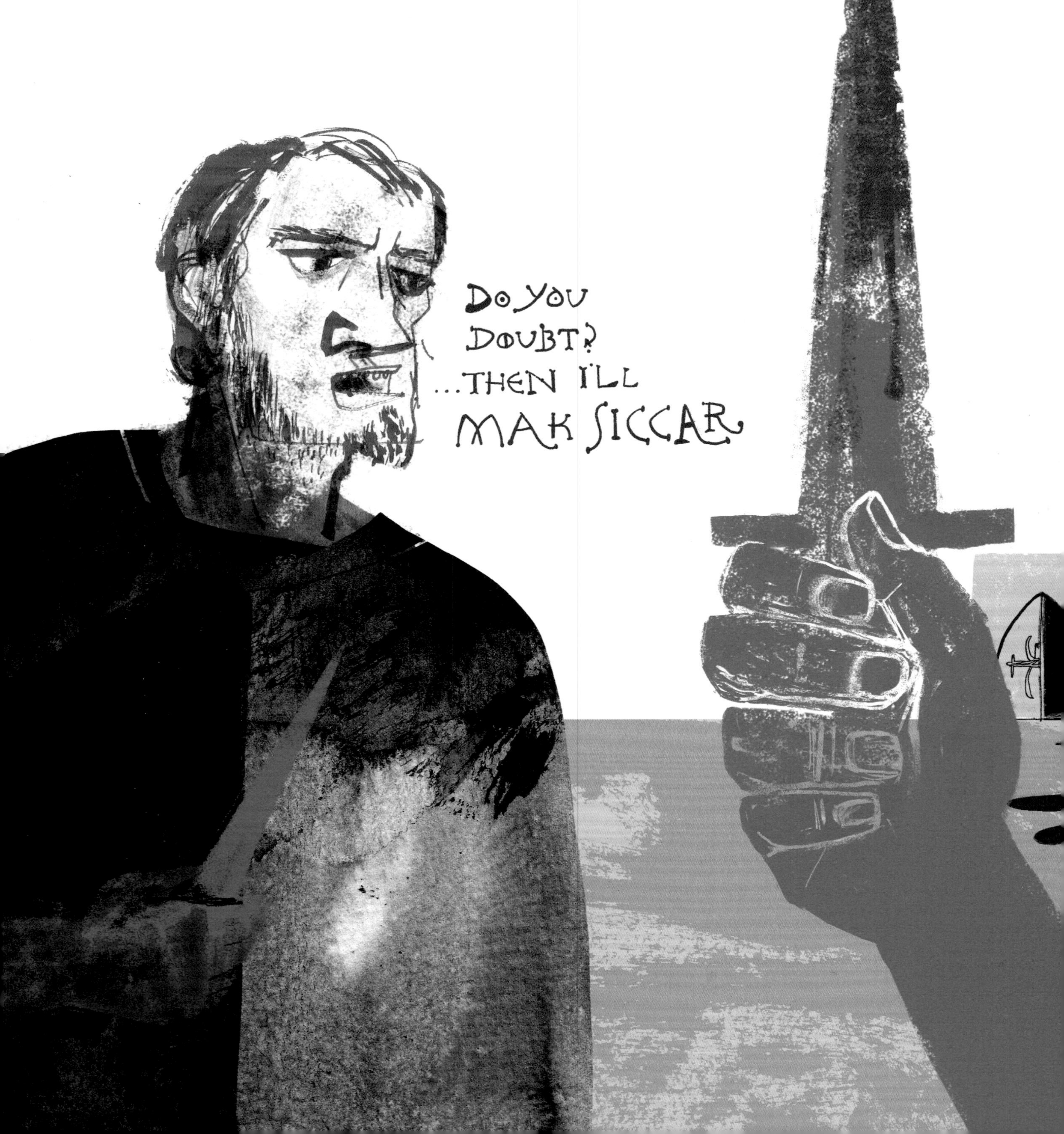
DO YOU DOUBT? ...THEN I'LL MAK SICCAR

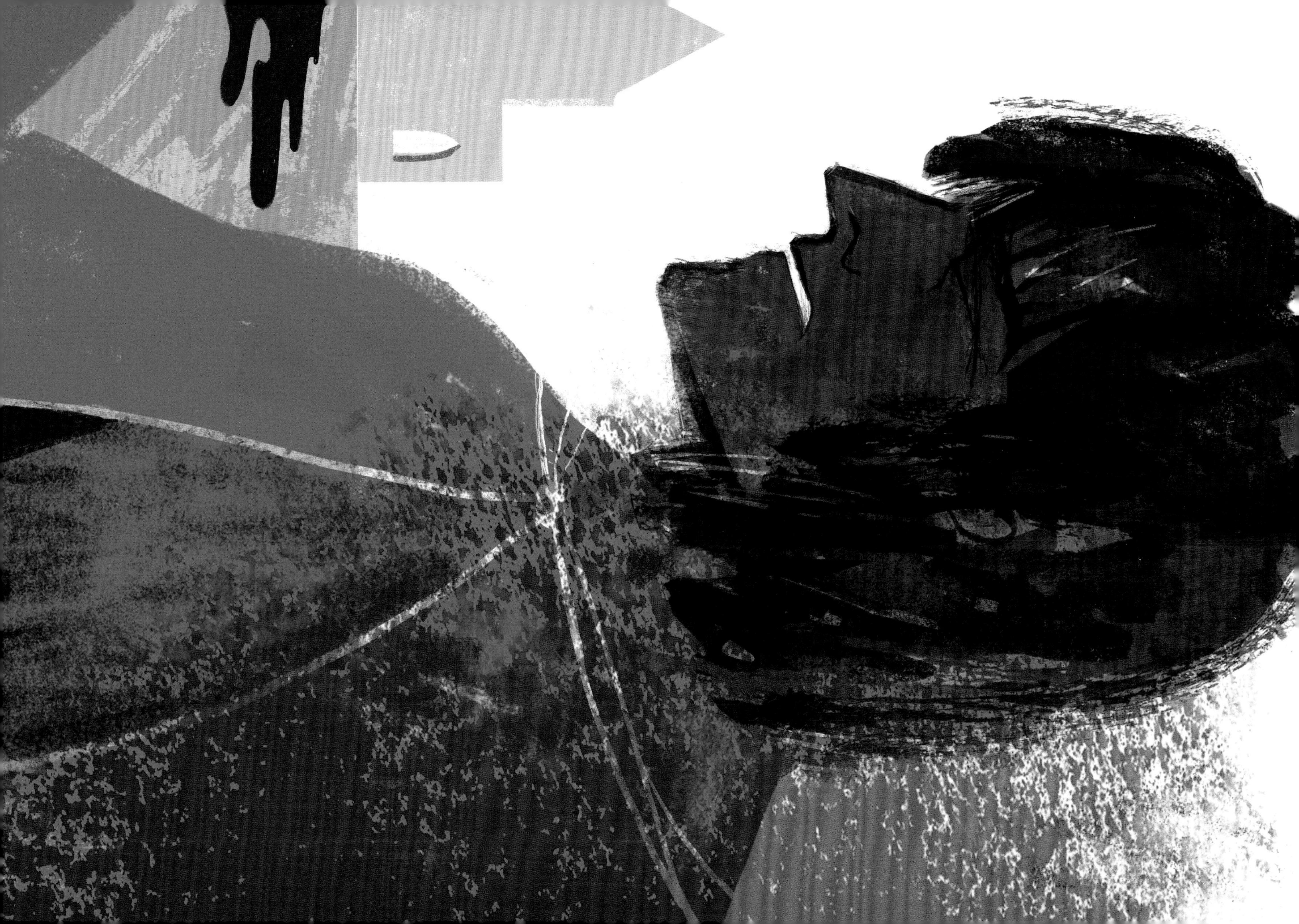

There was no going back from this sacrilegious deed. Men hurried to his side, and Bruce moved swiftly across the south-west, capturing and destroying castles. Six weeks later, at Scone, he was crowned King of Scots in the presence of three bishops, four earls and many other supporters. Among them was the nineteen-year-old Isabel, Countess of Buchan, whose husband's cousin Bruce had just murdered. Another of King Robert's firm supporters was a young knight, aged no more than twenty, called Sir James Douglas. His father, a staunch ally of William Wallace, had died a prisoner in the Tower of London. 'The Good Sir James', or 'the Black Douglas' as he was also known, soon became Bruce's most trusted comrade and, like the King himself, would prove himself a master of guerrilla warfare.

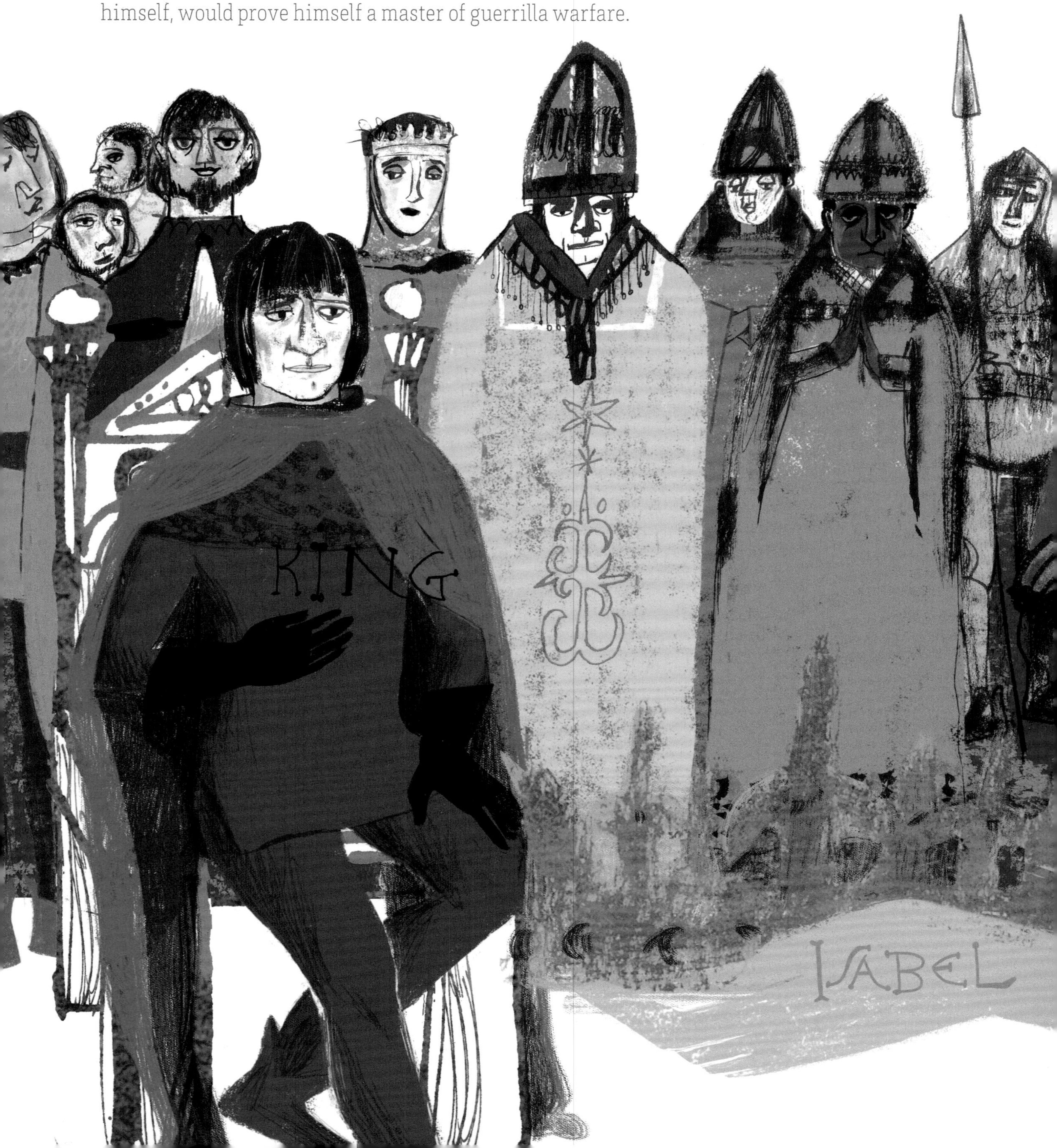
KING
ISABEL

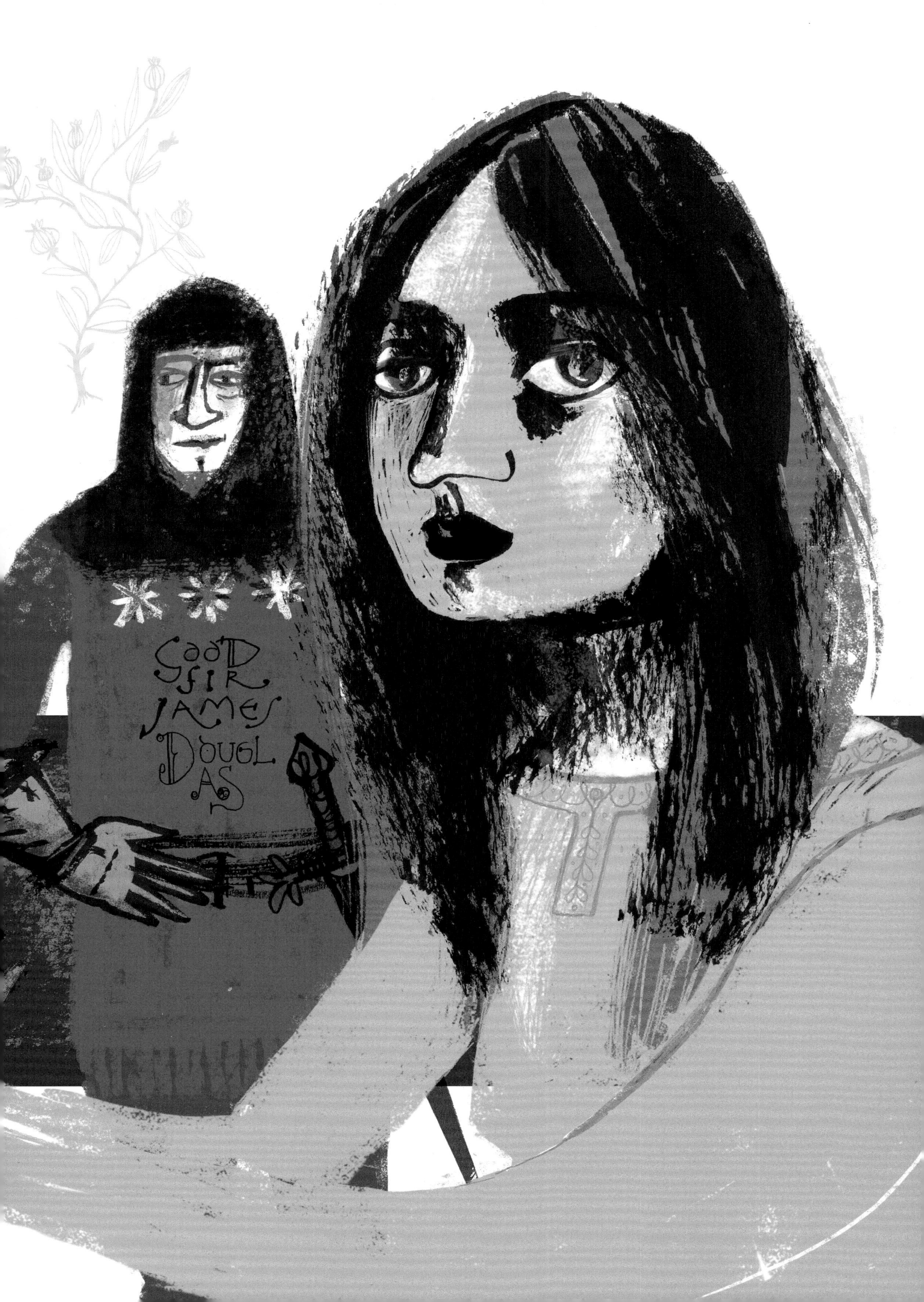
GOOD
SIR
JAMES
DOUGL
AS

Edward I gave orders for immediate retaliation against Bruce. On 18th June 1306 an English force surprised him in a dawn attack at Methven, seven miles west of Perth. Bruce fled westward, and near Tyndrum suffered a second defeat at the hands of the MacDougalls, who were related to the murdered Red Comyn. While Bruce and what was left of his force took to the mountains, his wife Elizabeth, daughter Marjorie and other women in the party went north under the protection of his brother Neil, hoping to escape to Orkney. But at Tain they were apprehended by the Earl of Ross (a supporter of John Balliol) and delivered into the hands of Edward I.

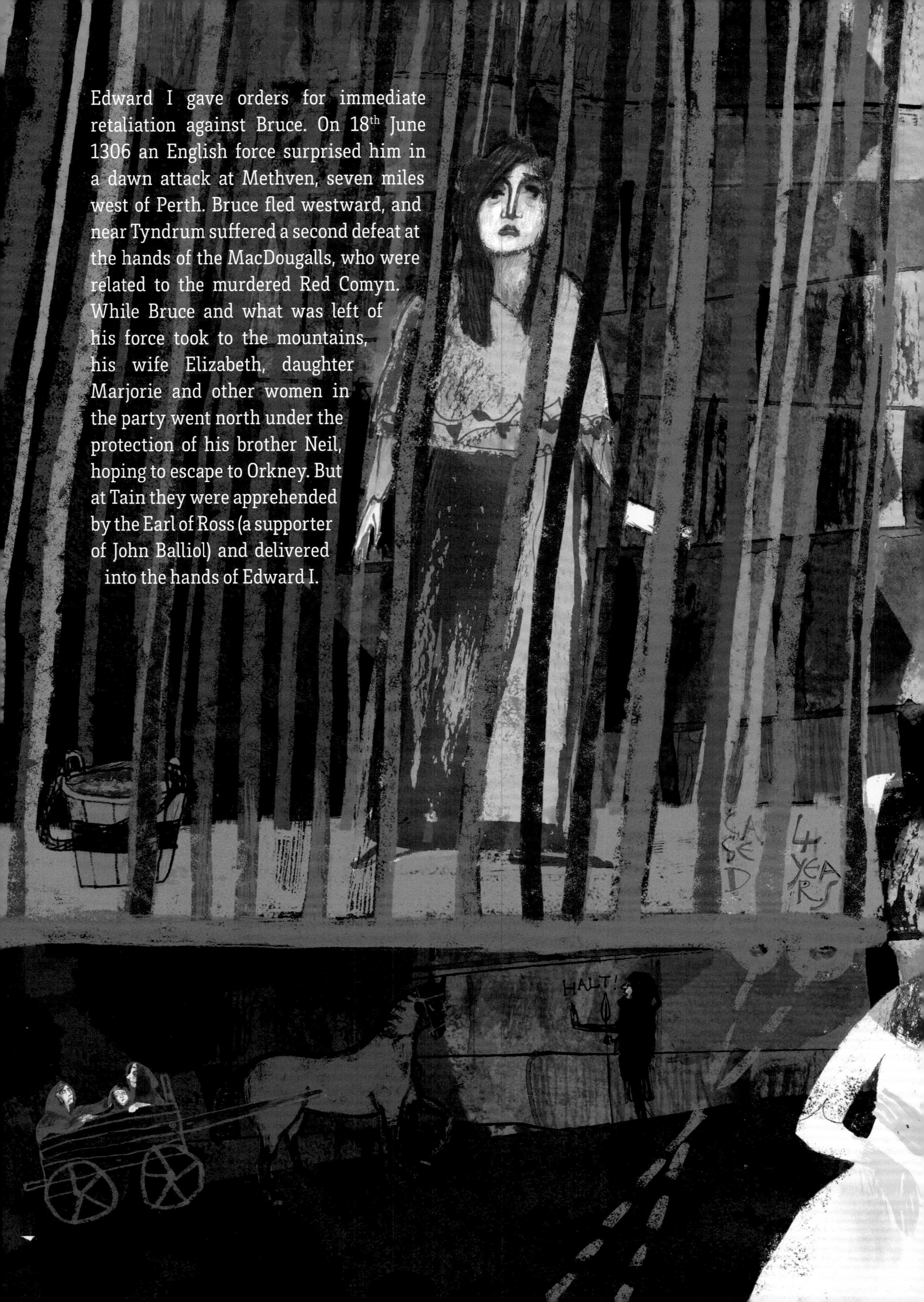
CAGED
4 YEARS
HALT!

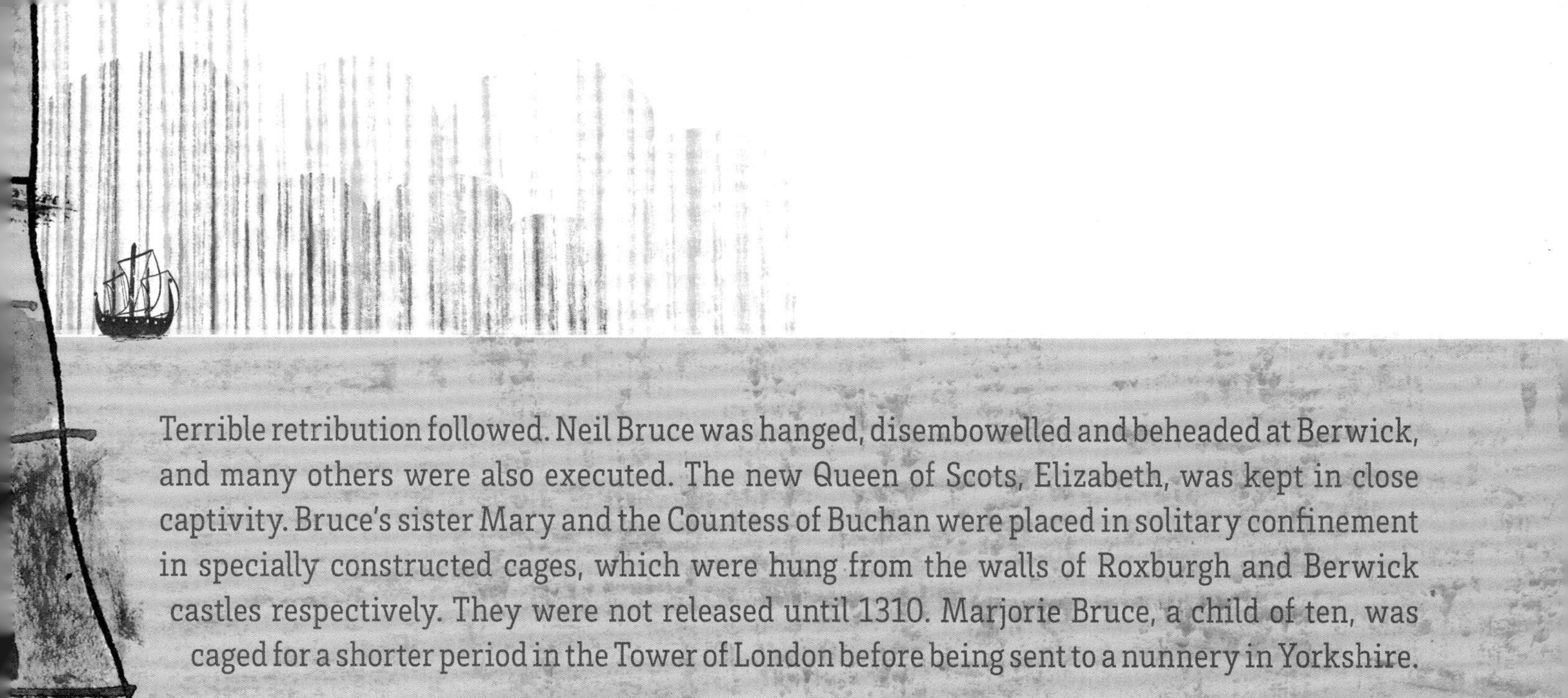

Terrible retribution followed. Neil Bruce was hanged, disembowelled and beheaded at Berwick, and many others were also executed. The new Queen of Scots, Elizabeth, was kept in close captivity. Bruce's sister Mary and the Countess of Buchan were placed in solitary confinement in specially constructed cages, which were hung from the walls of Roxburgh and Berwick castles respectively. They were not released until 1310. Marjorie Bruce, a child of ten, was caged for a shorter period in the Tower of London before being sent to a nunnery in Yorkshire.

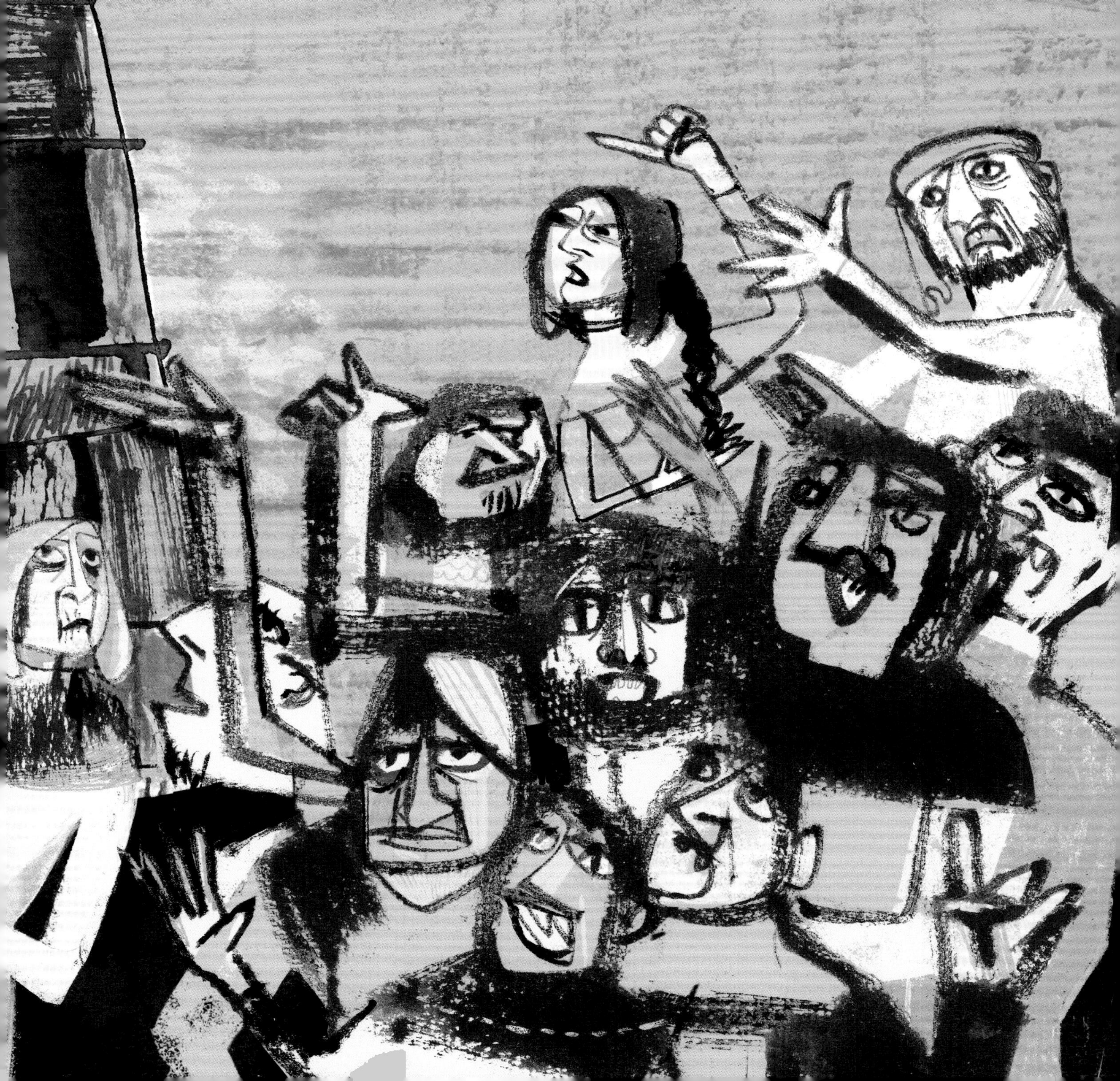

Robert Bruce, like William Wallace before him, was now a man on the run. He left the mainland and reputedly took refuge in the Hebrides, in Ireland, or on Rathlinn Island off the Antrim coast. It was from this period that the legend of his encounter with a spider grew. Pondering his bleak situation, Bruce is said to have watched a spider trying and repeatedly failing to spin its web. When it at last succeeded, the King was so impressed by its perseverance that he resolved to try once again to win freedom for Scotland, and Scotland for himself.

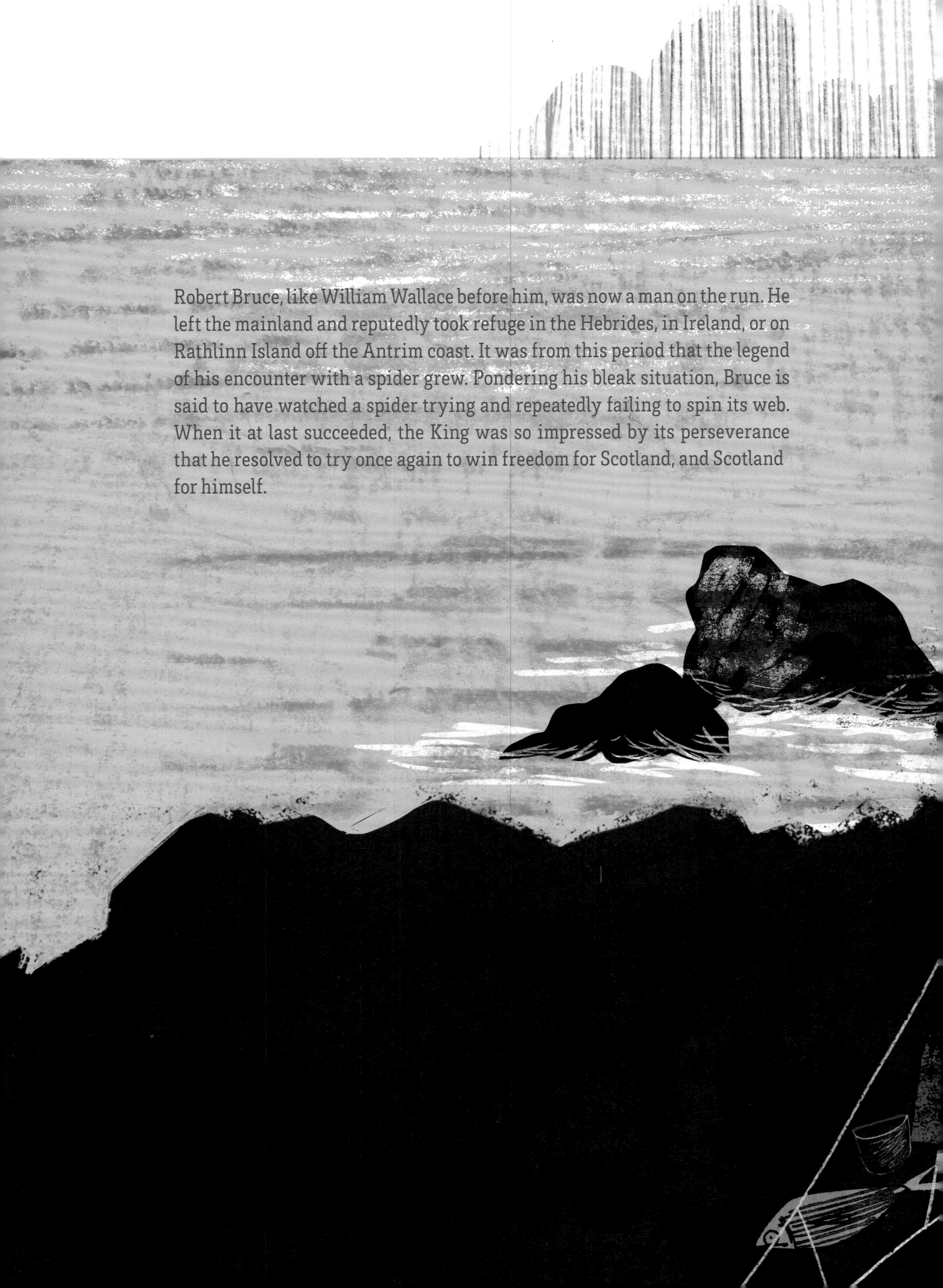

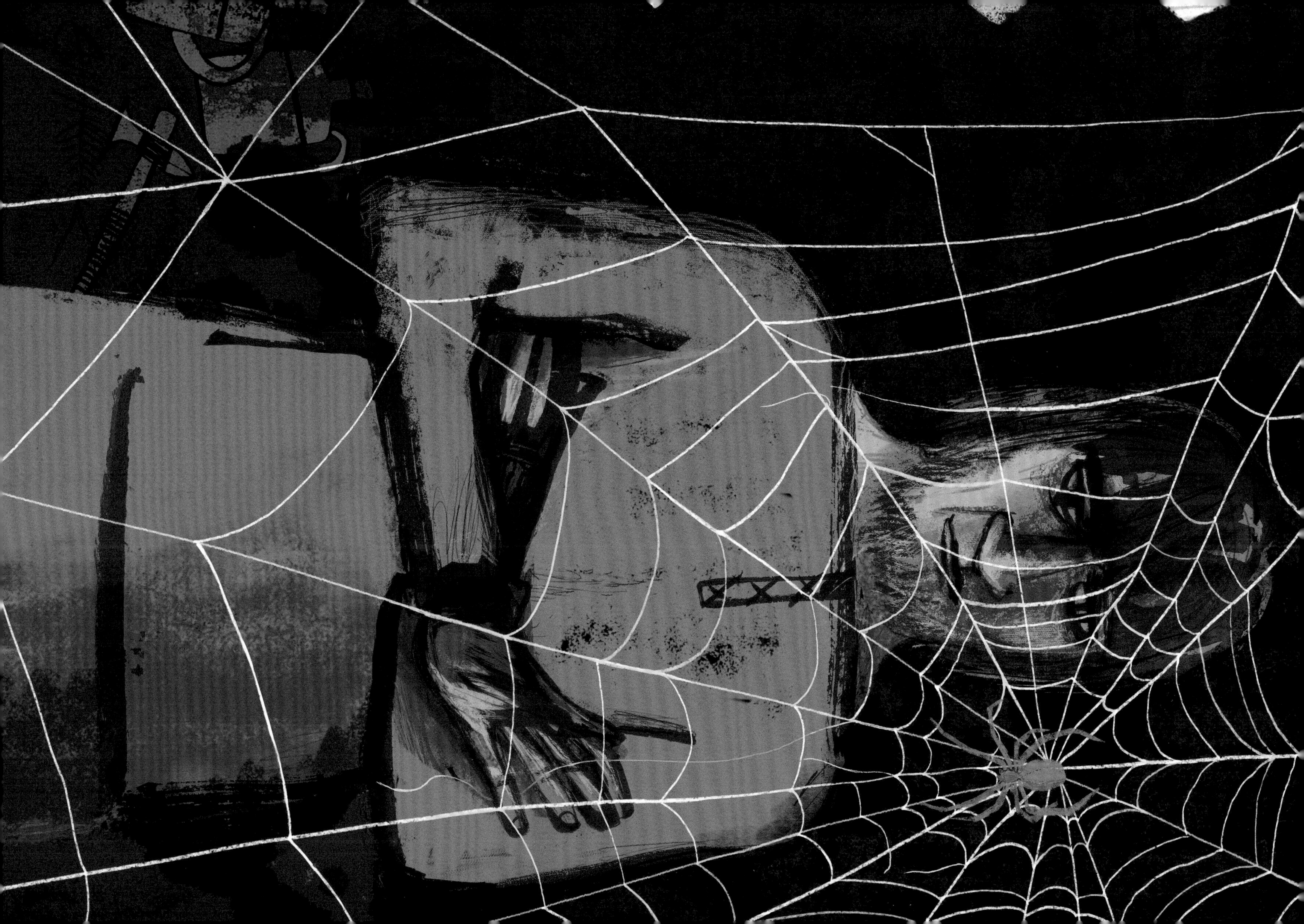

He had no army and little money, he was separated from his family, and most of his supporters were either imprisoned, dead or in hiding. Yet he believed his cause to be just. Having survived the winter of 1306–07, he gathered a band of Irishmen and Hebridean islanders, and landed in Kintyre. From there he moved to the Isle of Arran. Dividing his forces, he sent his brothers Thomas and Alexander to Galloway, while he planned an attack on his own birthplace, Turnberry Castle. A spy was sent ahead to estimate the strength of the English garrison. If he thought the castle could be captured, he was supposed to light a fire. He did not do so, but by chance another fire was lit which persuaded Bruce to come over from Arran. The castle was not taken, but in a night attack the Scots surprised a large number of English soldiers in the nearby village, killing them all.

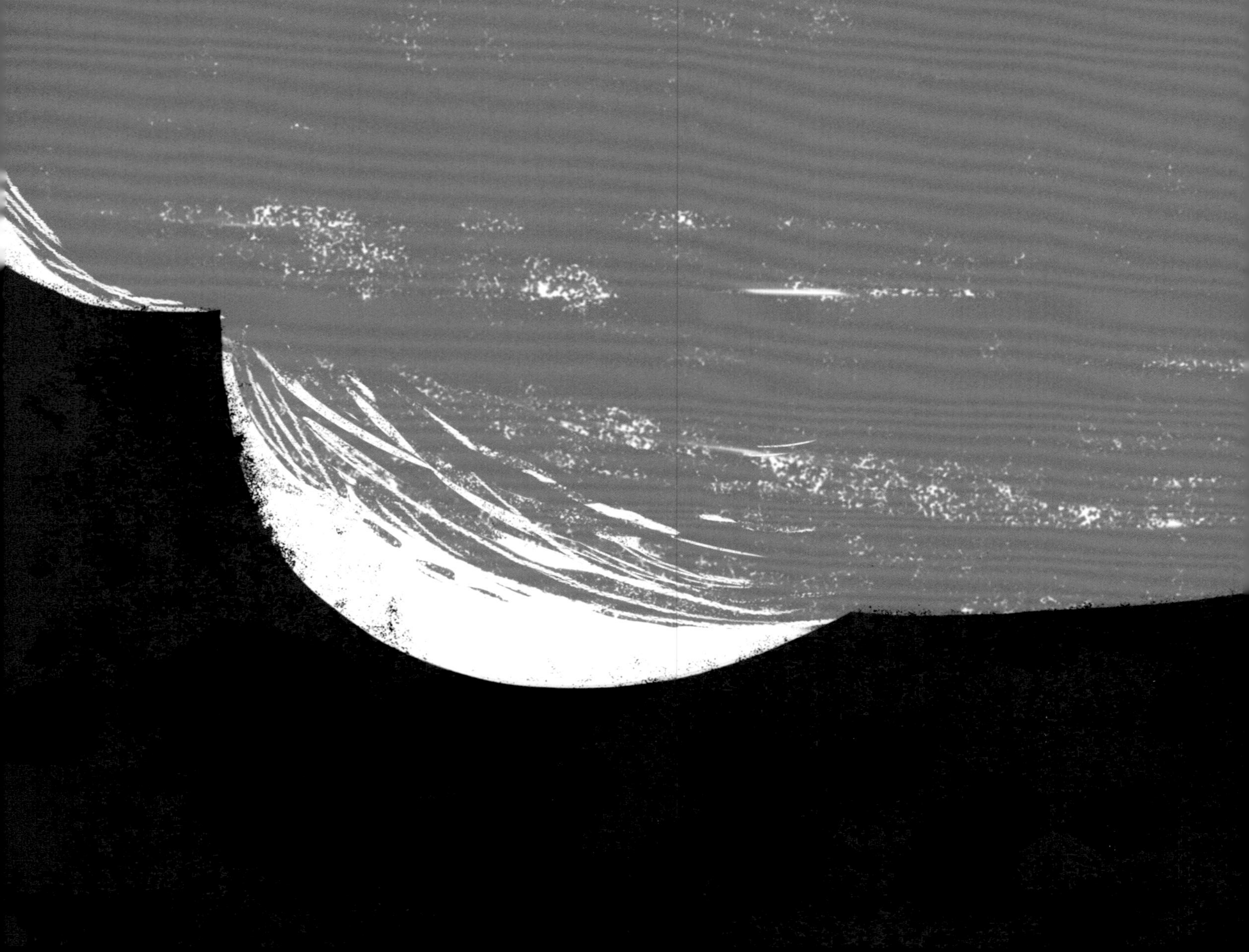

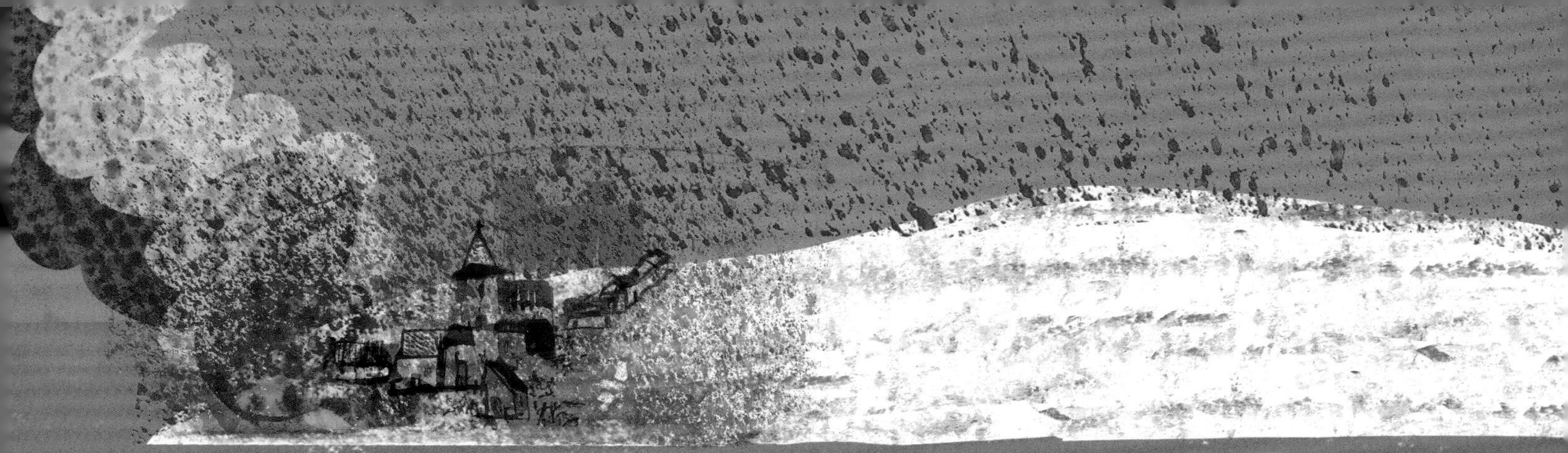

Thomas and Alexander Bruce's Galloway expedition, however, ended in total defeat. The two wounded brothers were sent to Carlisle, and there, on the orders of the now ailing King Edward, they were hanged and beheaded.

Bruce now abandoned the chivalric mode of warfare in which, as a knight and a nobleman, he had been schooled from boyhood. He understood that he would never defeat the English, with their superior wealth and manpower, by such means. For the next seven years he avoided pitched battles and long sieges, relying on mobility, surprise and hit-and-run attacks. He dismantled any fortress that fell into his hands.

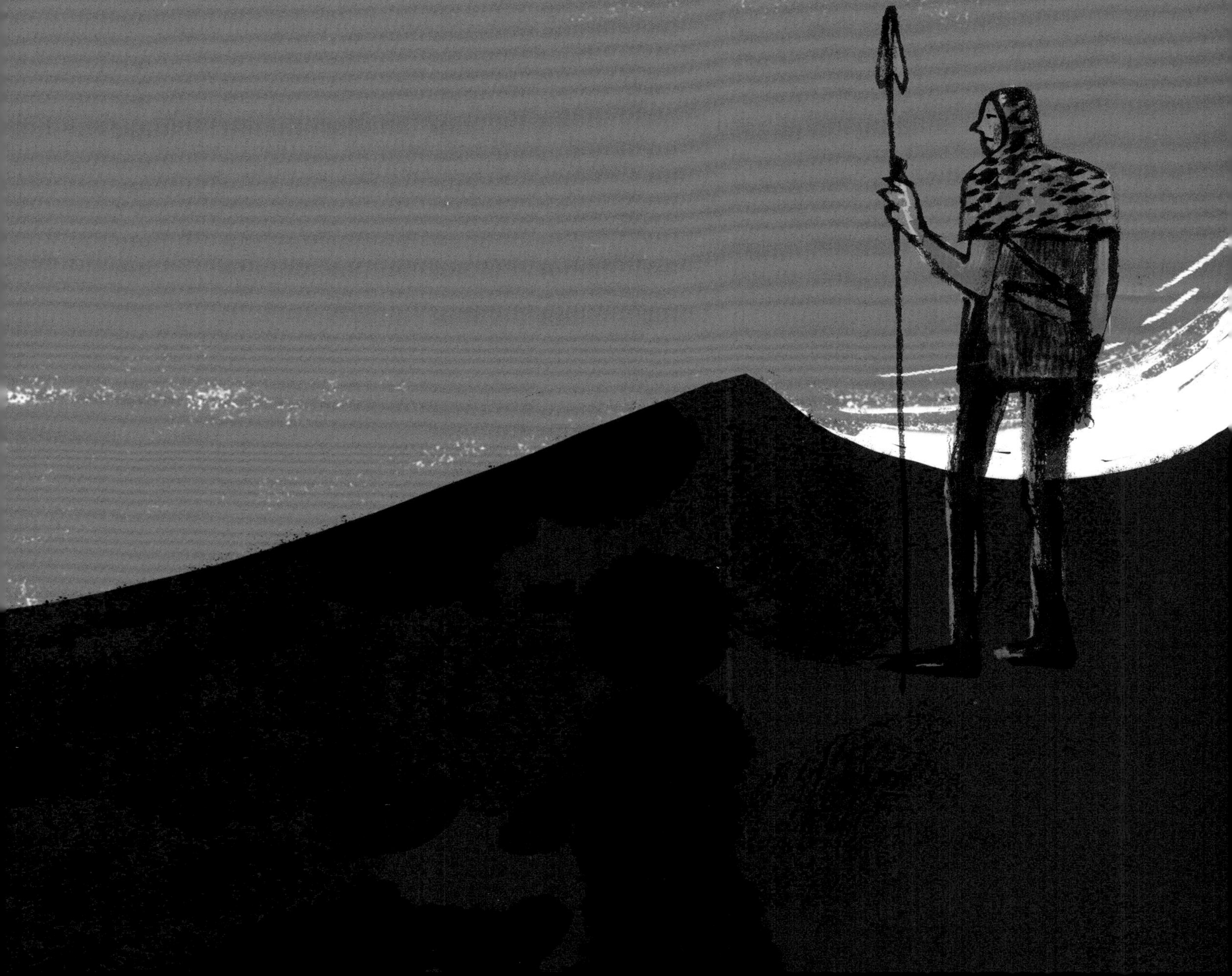

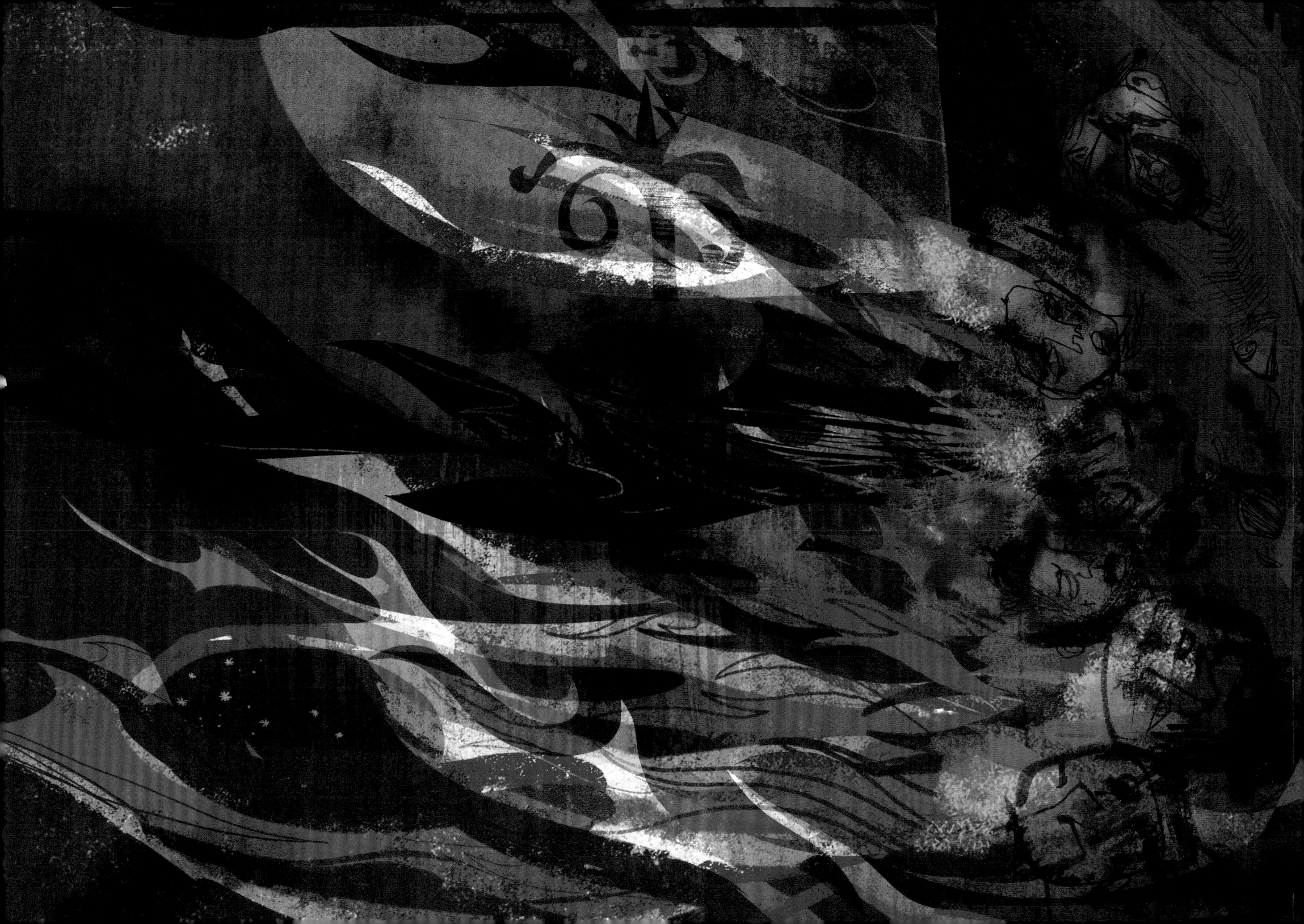

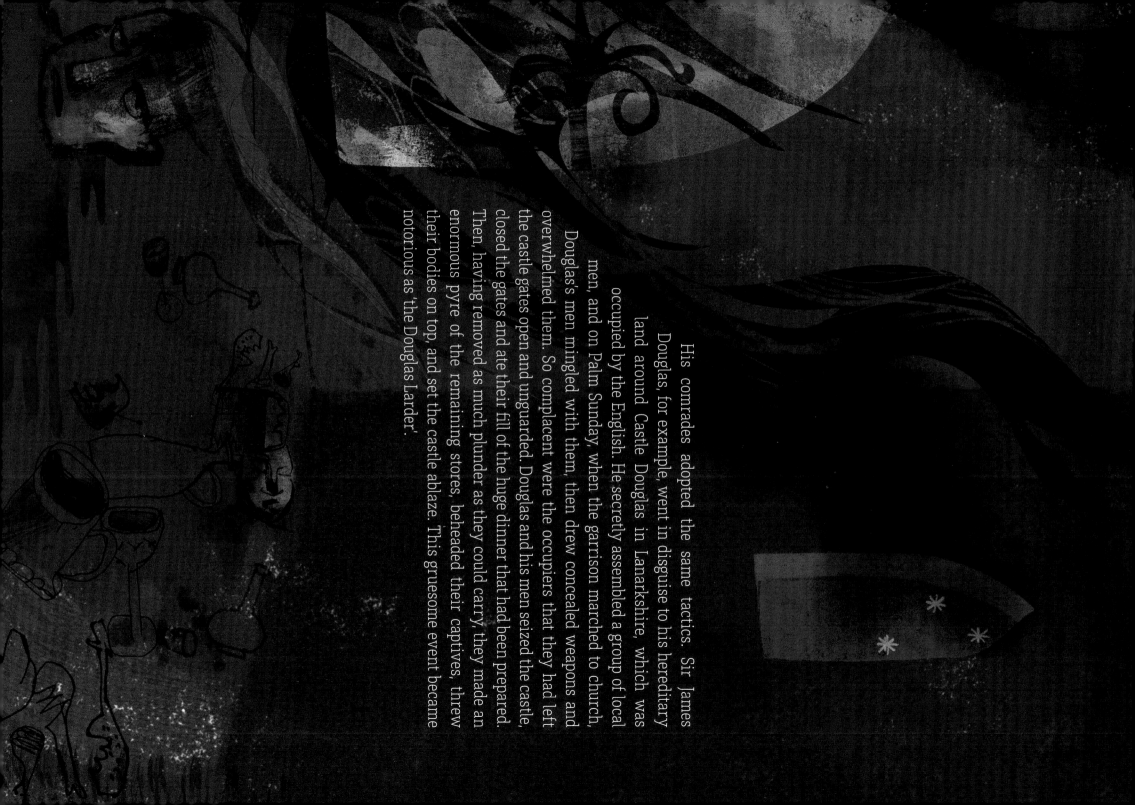

His comrades adopted the same tactics. Sir James Douglas, for example, went in disguise to his hereditary land around Castle Douglas in Lanarkshire, which was occupied by the English. He secretly assembled a group of local men, and on Palm Sunday, when the garrison marched to church, Douglas's men mingled with them, then drew concealed weapons and overwhelmed them. So complacent were the occupiers that they had left the castle gates open and unguarded. Douglas and his men seized the castle, closed the gates and ate their fill of the huge dinner that had been prepared. Then, having removed as much plunder as they could carry, they made an enormous pyre of the remaining stores, beheaded their captives, threw their bodies on top, and set the castle ablaze. This gruesome event became notorious as 'the Douglas Larder'.

Bruce meanwhile, with 300 men, disappeared into the wilds of Glen Trool in Galloway, lured his English pursuers after him and then ambushed and defeated them. He advanced north, met another English force at Loudoun Hill in Ayrshire and routed it. Three days later he won another victory near Ayr.

This was in May 1307. Two months later Edward I died. Far from crushing the Scots, his policy of repression had driven many to take up arms against him, convinced that only Robert Bruce could win them freedom and peace.

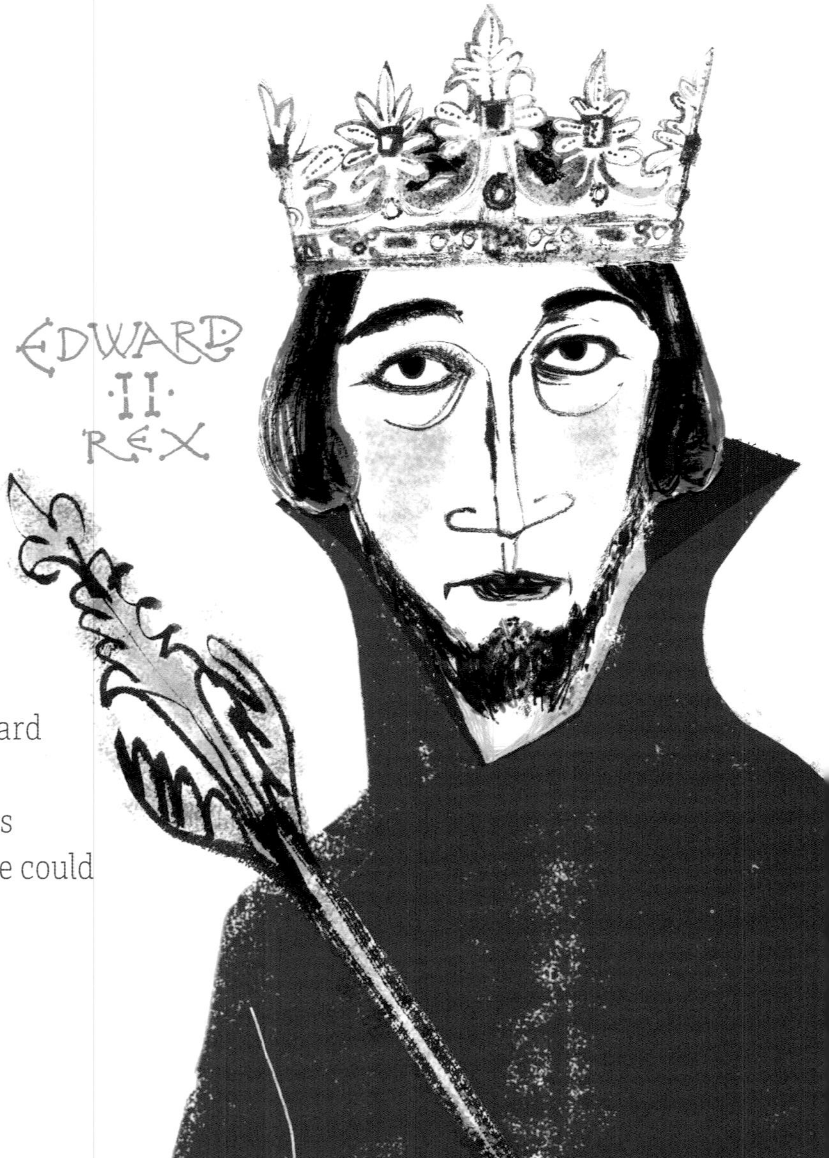
EDWARD
·II·
REX

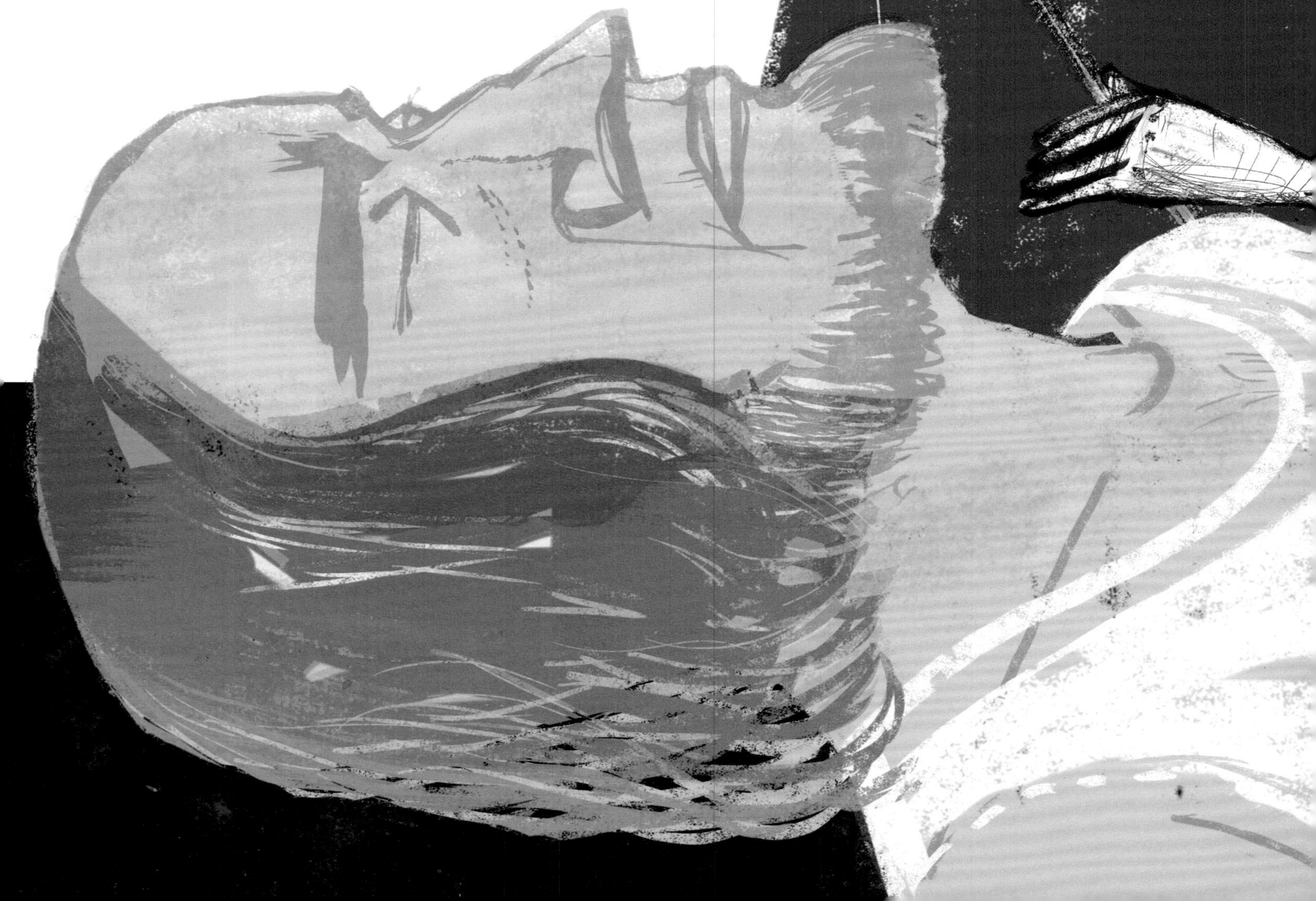

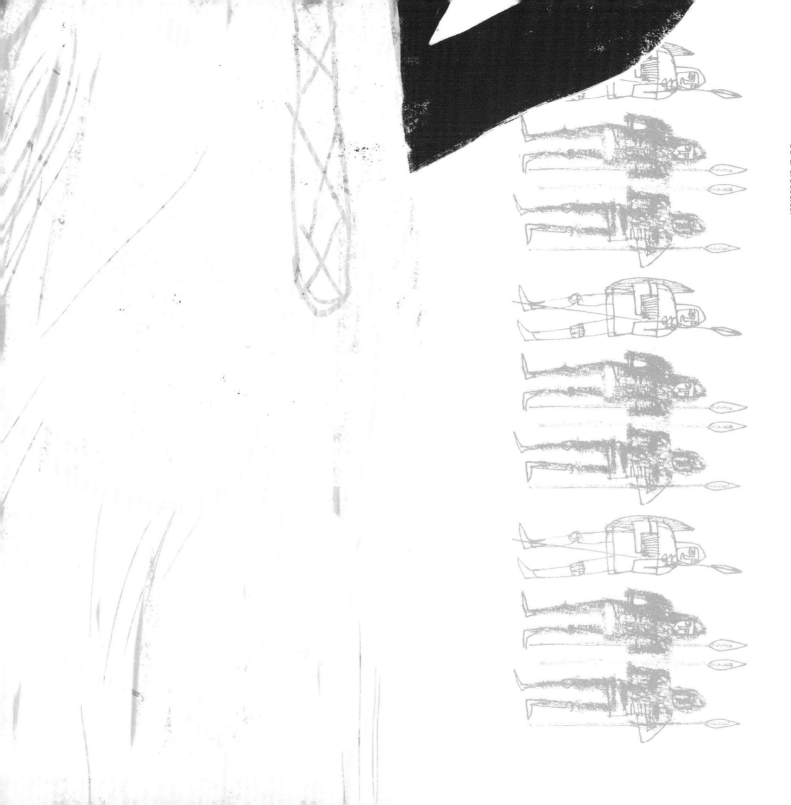

The new English king, Edward II, was neither as determined nor as ruthless as his father. After an ineffective summer campaign he retired to England and did not come north of the Border again for three years. The English commanders left behind had no appetite for taking the fight to the Scots, preferring the safety of their castles. This allowed Bruce to attack the Scots lords still ranged against him. Sir James Douglas secured the south of the country, while Bruce moved north to confront his old rival John Comyn, Earl of Buchan.

At Inverurie the trials and strains of recent months caught up with Bruce and he fell so seriously ill that it was feared he would die. Winter arrived, and with it snow and a shortage of food for his army of 700. Buchan closed in for the kill, but Bruce, rising from his sickbed, led his force into battle and won the day. The Earl fled to England and died soon after. His earldom was laid waste by Bruce's men: crops were burned, cattle slaughtered and the whole territory so reduced that it could not pose a future threat.

Bruce now turned his attention to either destroying or winning over his other great foe in the north, the Earl of Ross. The Earl appealed for help from Edward II, but when no help was sent Ross made terms and changed sides, and became one of Bruce's firmest allies.

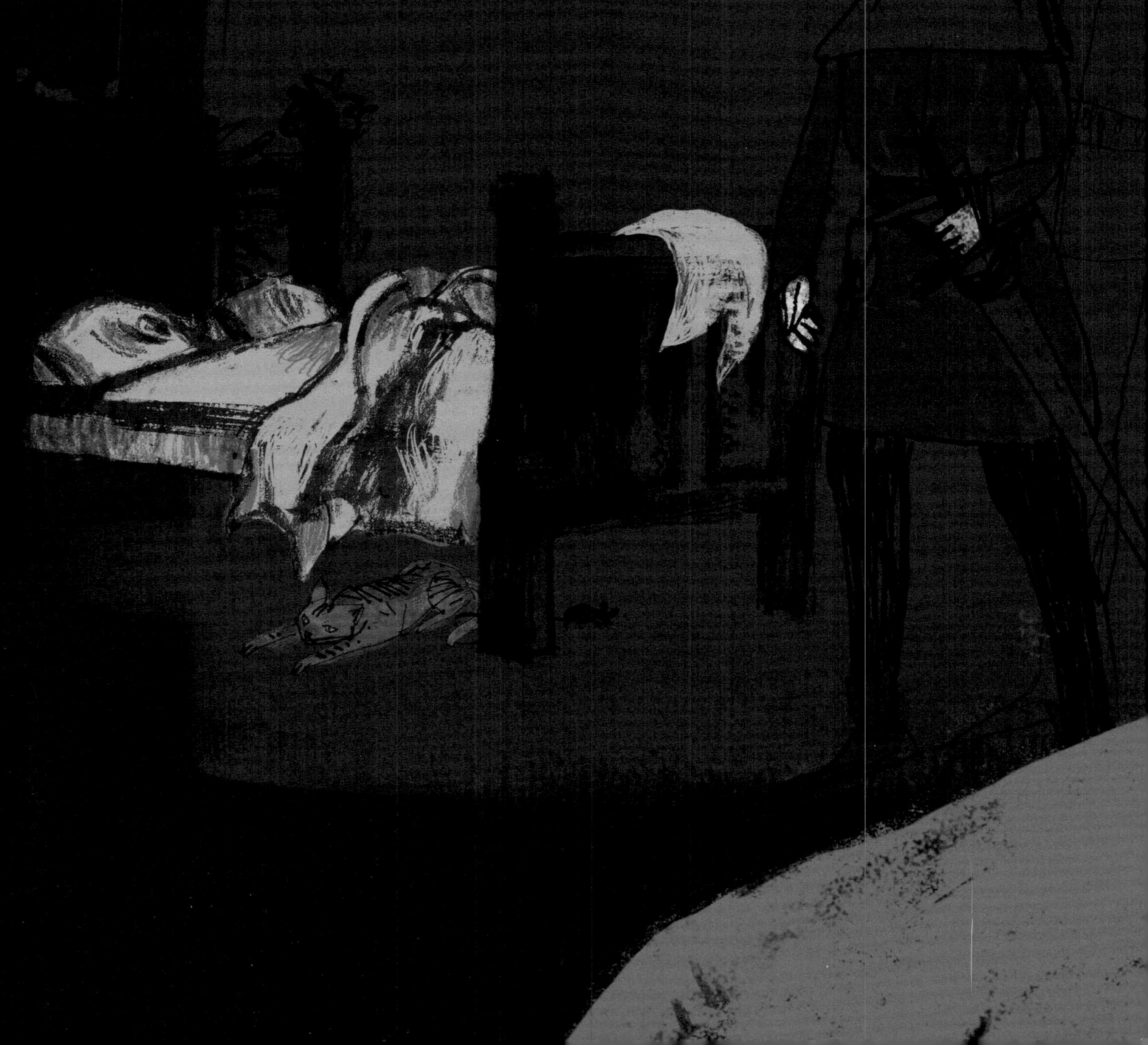

With the north now under control, Robert was able to attack the MacDougalls, penetrating deep into their Argyll homeland. At Loch Awe, where the steep and narrow Pass of Brander runs between the loch and the slopes of Ben Cruachan, the MacDougalls lay in wait, hoping to trap Bruce's army in the pass. But Bruce sent a body of men under Sir James Douglas to outflank the enemy higher up the mountain, and when the MacDougalls launched their assault, firing arrows and rolling boulders down on the main army, they suddenly found themselves under similar attack from above. The men of Argyll broke and retreated, so hurriedly that they did not have time to destroy the only bridge across the River Awe, and Bruce followed all the way to Dunstaffnage Castle, which he soon took and demolished.

Meanwhile, his only surviving brother Edward carried out a fierce campaign into Galloway, which was still largely loyal to John Balliol. By the end of 1308, all the provinces most opposed to Bruce's cause had succumbed.

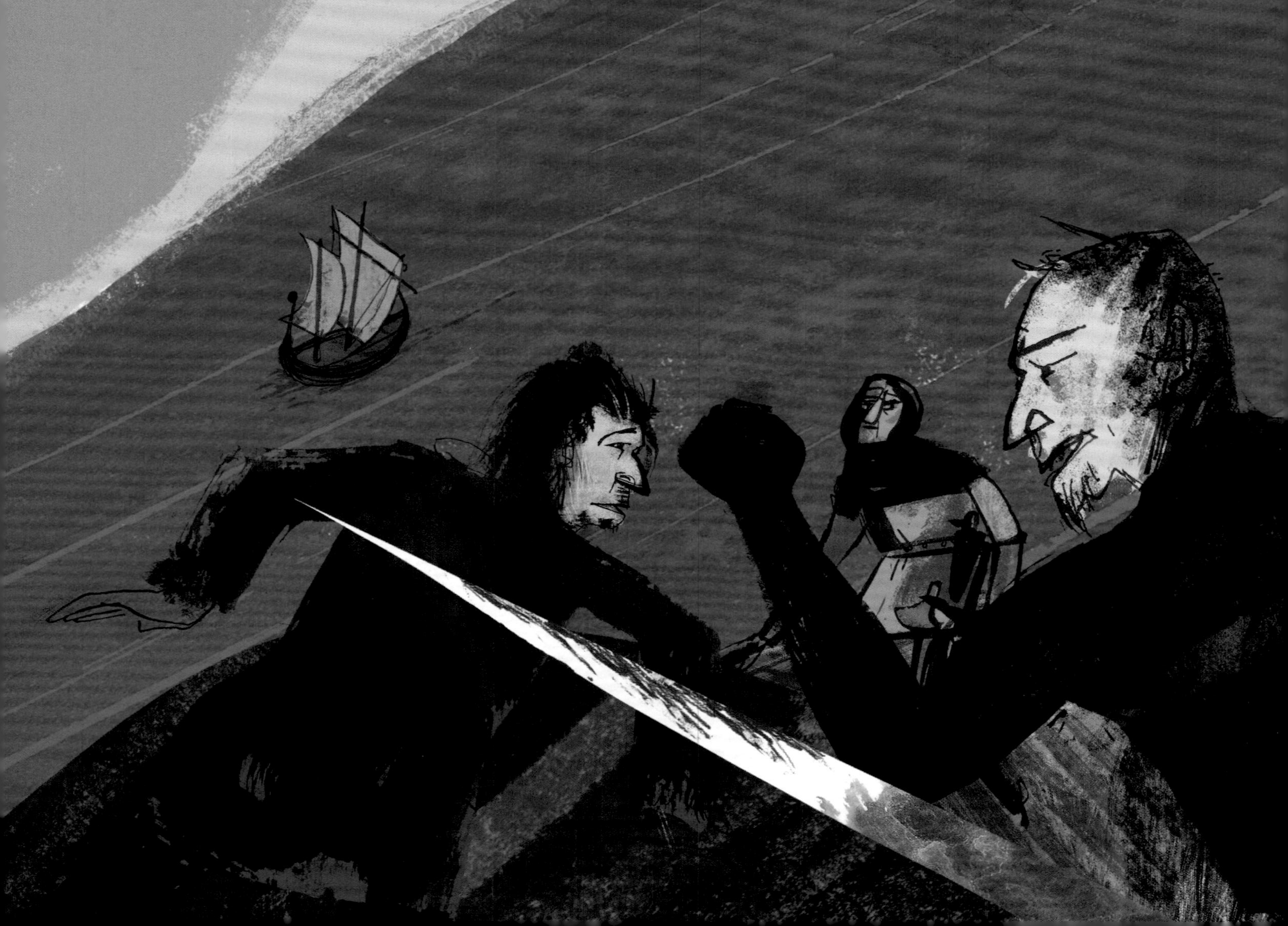

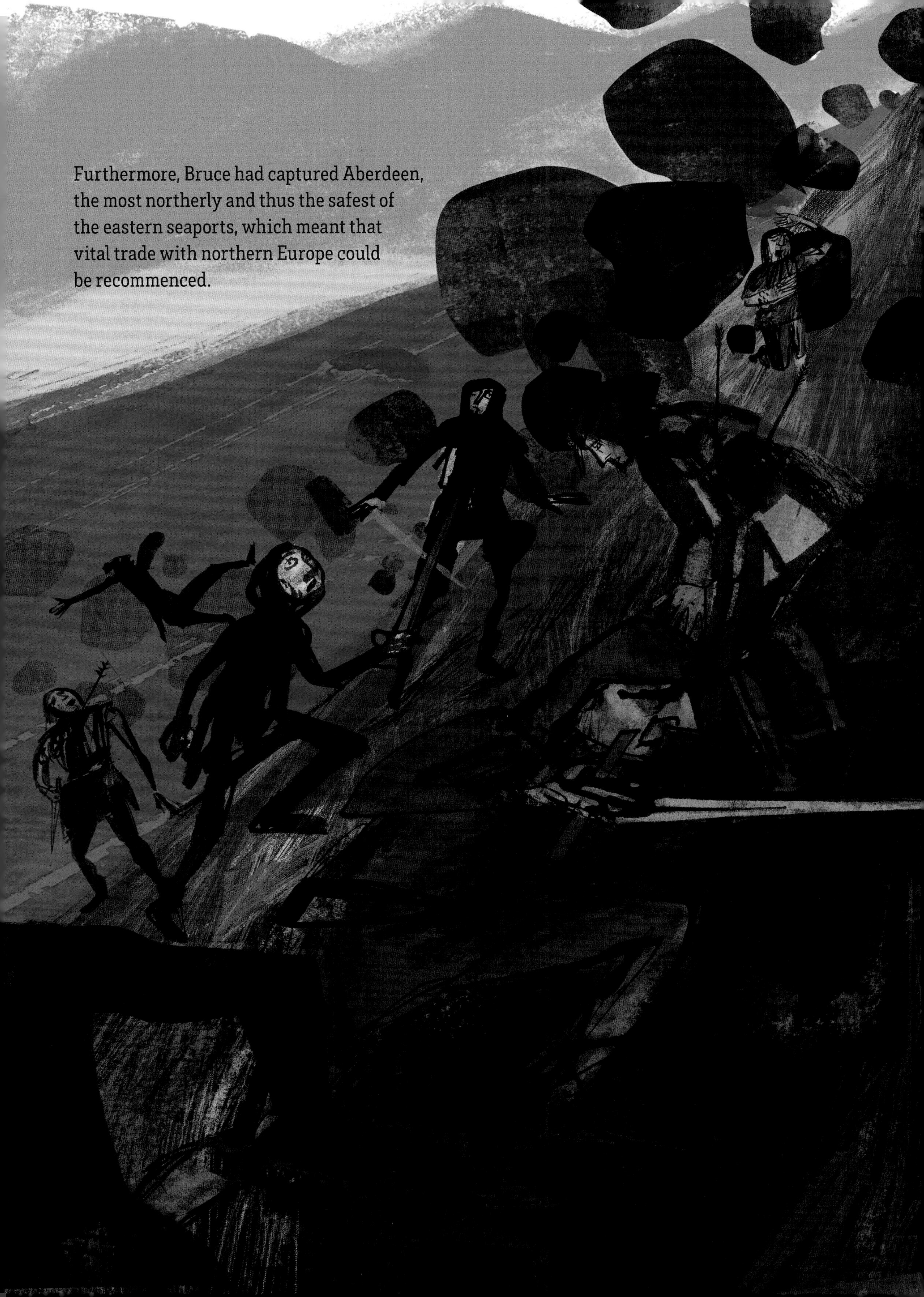

Furthermore, Bruce had captured Aberdeen, the most northerly and thus the safest of the eastern seaports, which meant that vital trade with northern Europe could be recommenced.

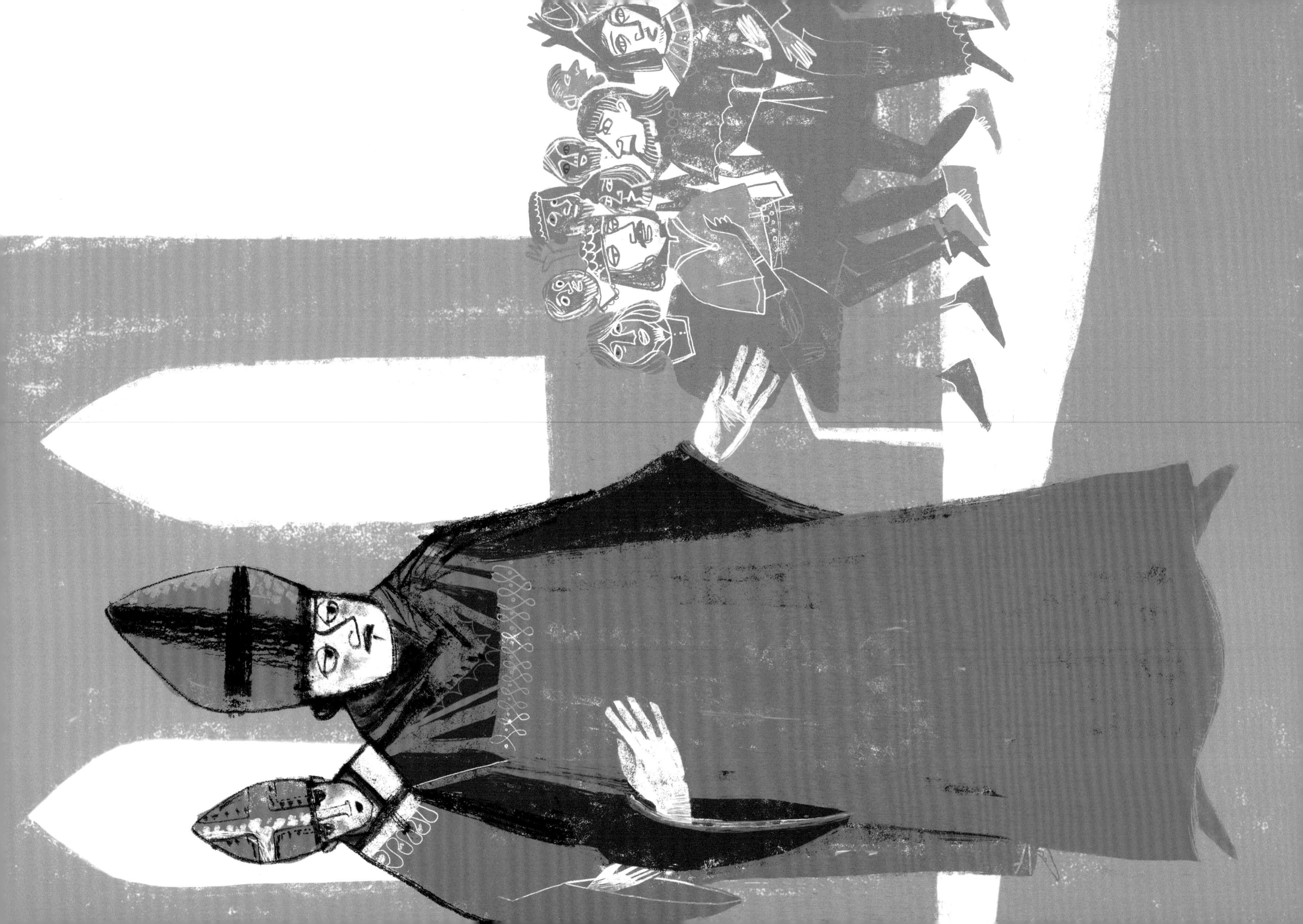

In March 1309 King Robert held his first parliament, at St Andrews. Cordial relations were re-established with Philip IV of France, and the Scottish bishops and nobility made declarations of loyalty to King Robert and to Scotland as an independent nation. Still, many castles remained in English hands, and five more years would pass before most of them were captured.

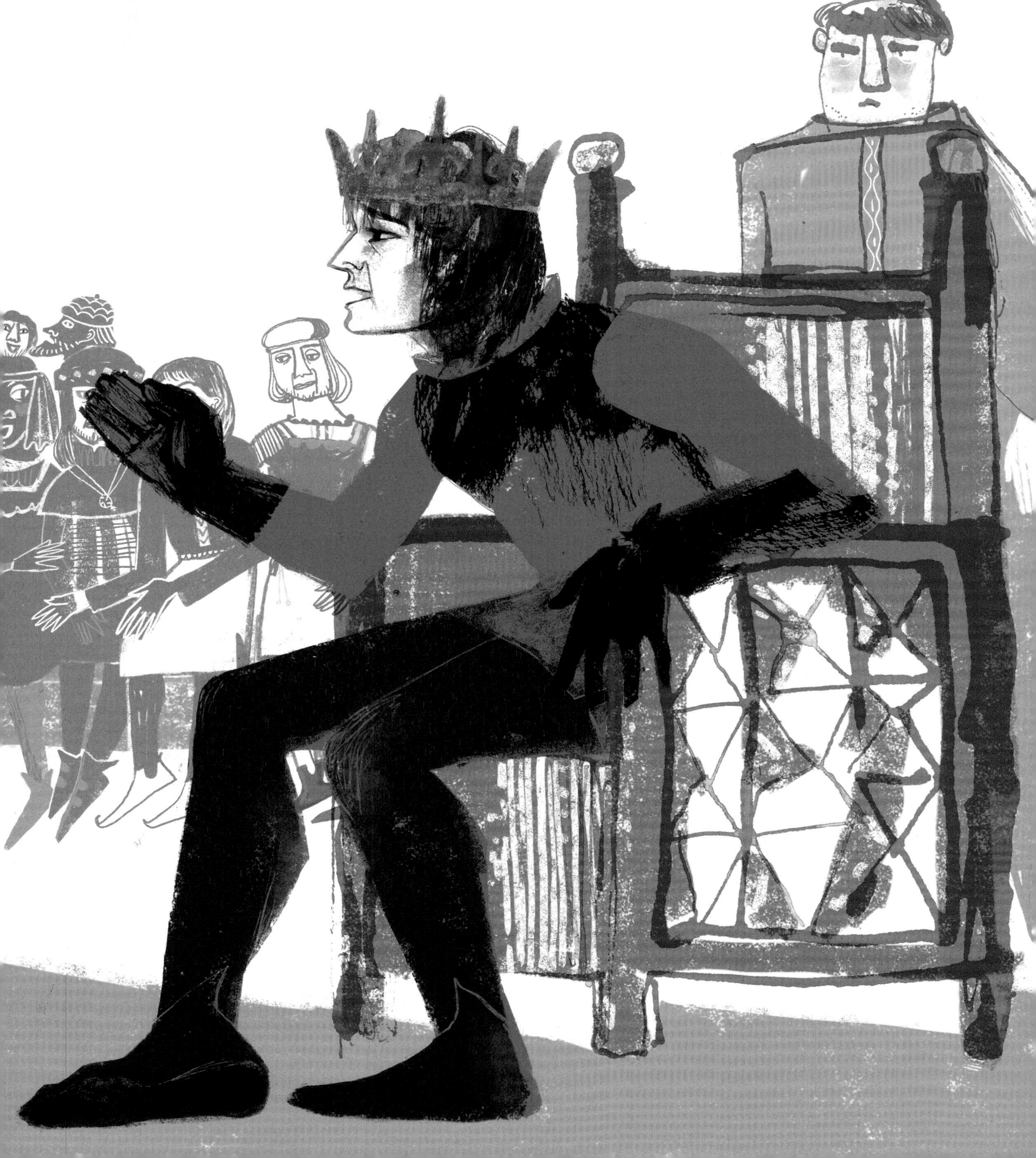

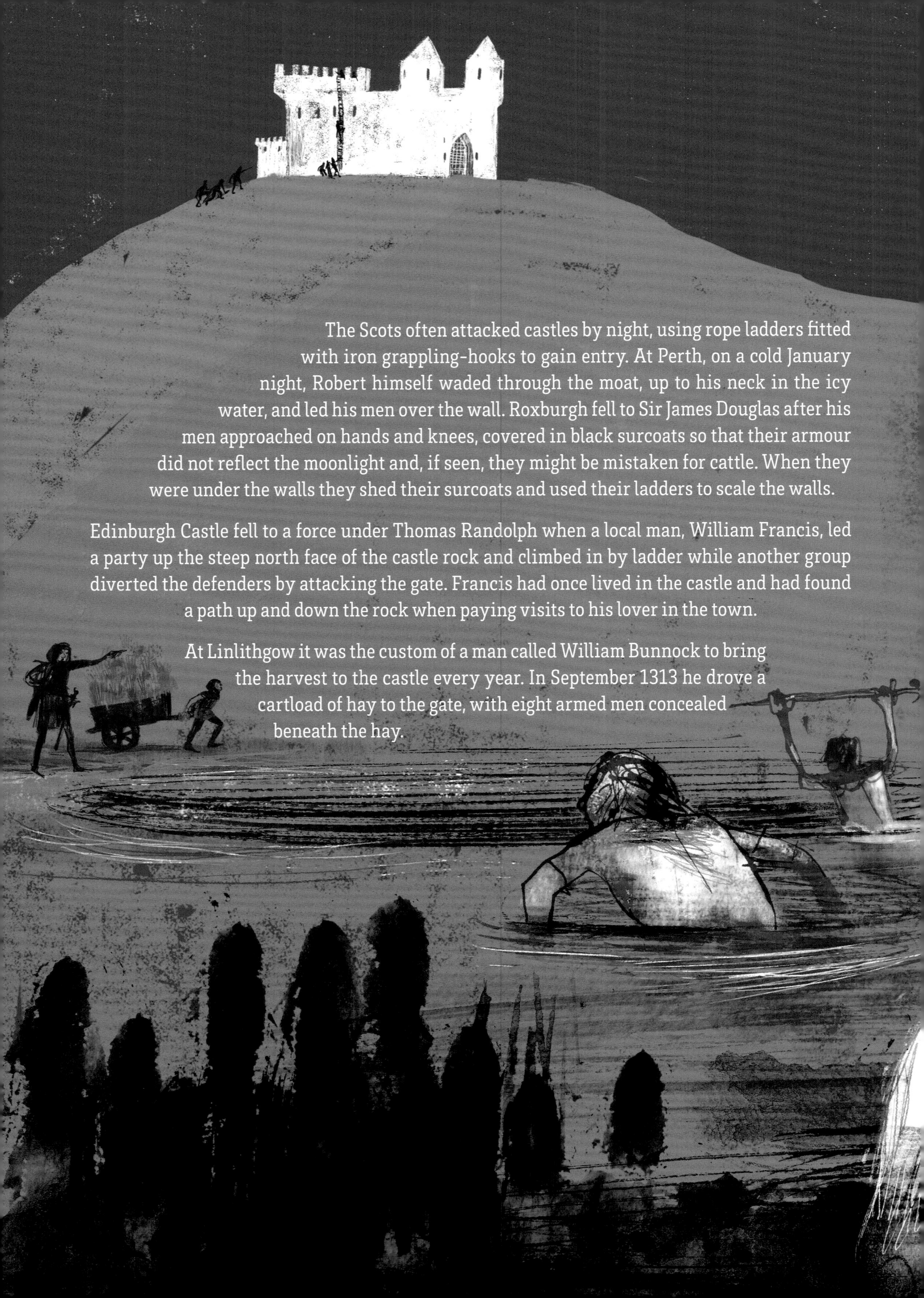

The Scots often attacked castles by night, using rope ladders fitted with iron grappling-hooks to gain entry. At Perth, on a cold January night, Robert himself waded through the moat, up to his neck in the icy water, and led his men over the wall. Roxburgh fell to Sir James Douglas after his men approached on hands and knees, covered in black surcoats so that their armour did not reflect the moonlight and, if seen, they might be mistaken for cattle. When they were under the walls they shed their surcoats and used their ladders to scale the walls.

Edinburgh Castle fell to a force under Thomas Randolph when a local man, William Francis, led a party up the steep north face of the castle rock and climbed in by ladder while another group diverted the defenders by attacking the gate. Francis had once lived in the castle and had found a path up and down the rock when paying visits to his lover in the town.

At Linlithgow it was the custom of a man called William Bunnock to bring the harvest to the castle every year. In September 1313 he drove a cartload of hay to the gate, with eight armed men concealed beneath the hay.

When the portcullis was raised he halted directly beneath it and cut the horses' traces so that the cart prevented the portcullis from falling. The hidden men emerged and secured the gate until reinforcements arrived and overwhelmed the garrison.

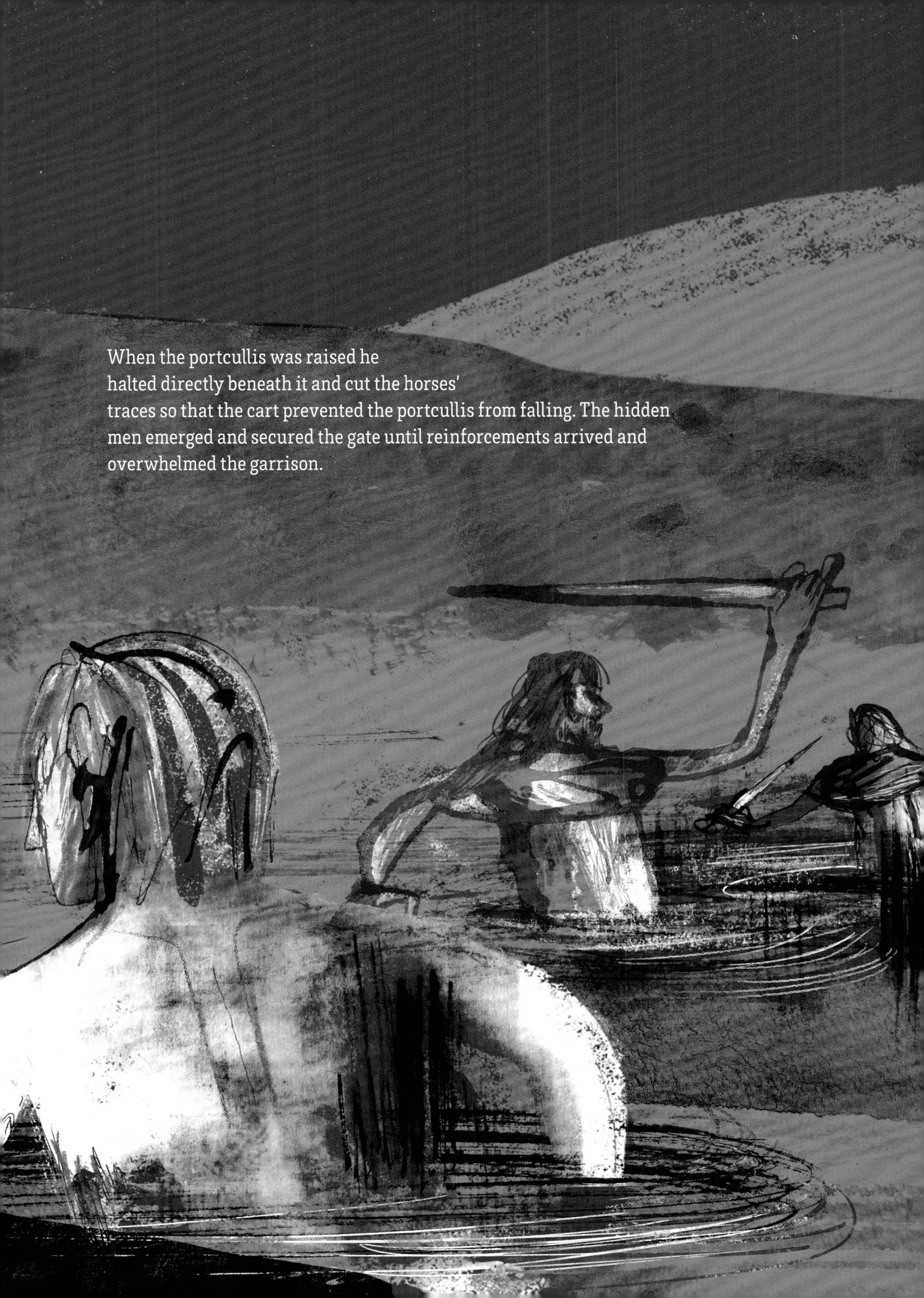

Thus by different methods nearly all of Scotland's strongholds fell to Bruce by early 1314. On each occasion, following his by now usual policy, he caused the castle to be razed. The one castle of strategic importance left in English hands was Stirling. Robert's brother Edward had rashly made a bargain with the garrison commander, Sir Philip Mowbray, at midsummer 1313: if Stirling were not relieved by the English king a year from that date Mowbray would surrender it. Robert was angry with his brother for striking this deal, and especially for giving Edward II such a long deadline. For years Bruce had avoided set-piece battles. Now, it seemed as if he might have to engage in just such a fight.

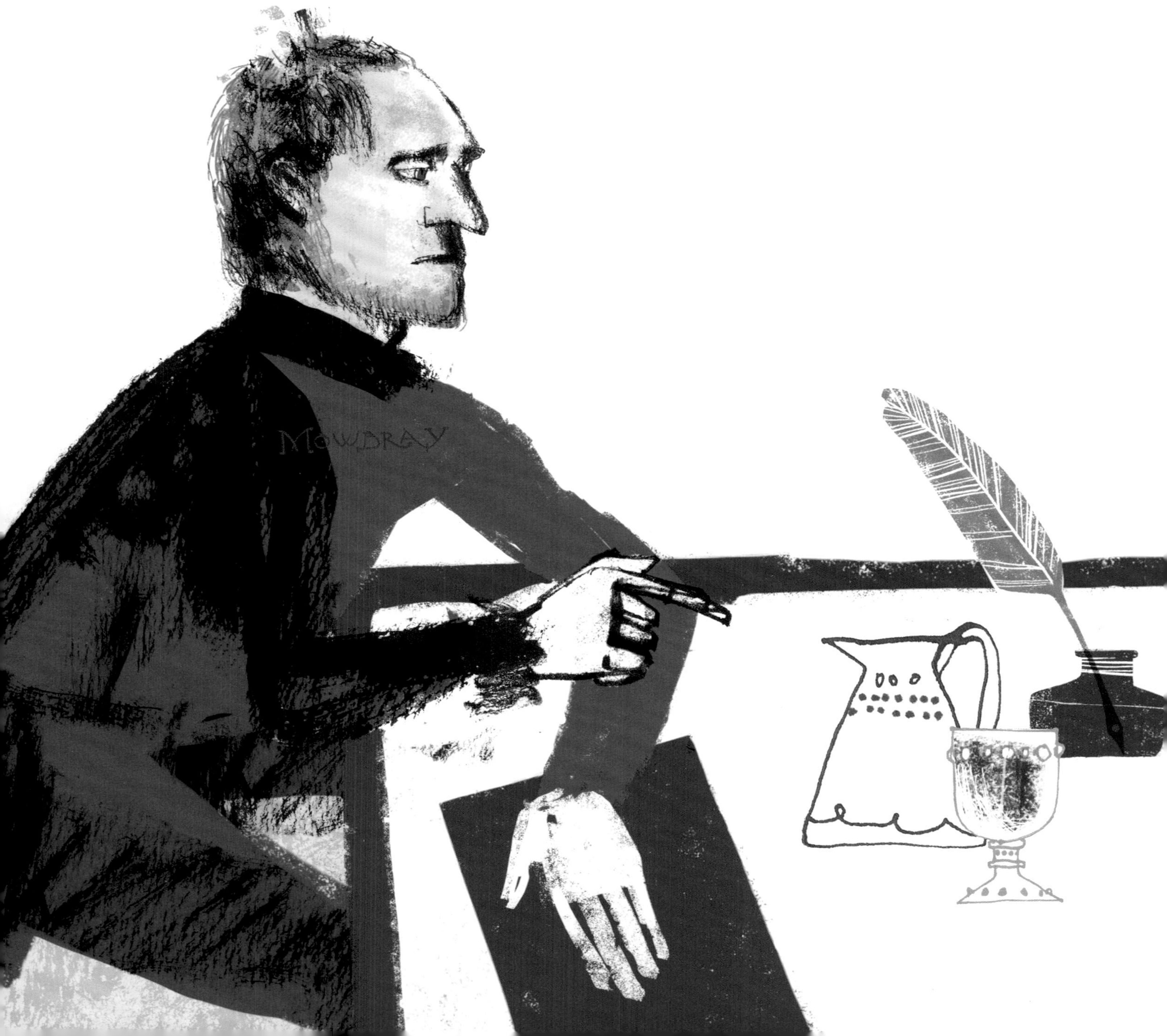
MOWBRAY

In the spring of 1314 Edward began to organise a huge army. He summoned footsoldiers and archers from Wales, Ireland and all the shires of England, and knights from as far afield as Gascony. Ships transported much of this army, which assembled at Berwick on 10 June. From there more than 15,000 infantry and some 2,500 heavy cavalry set off for Stirling, accompanied by a train of wagons, laden with food and equipment, that stretched for miles.

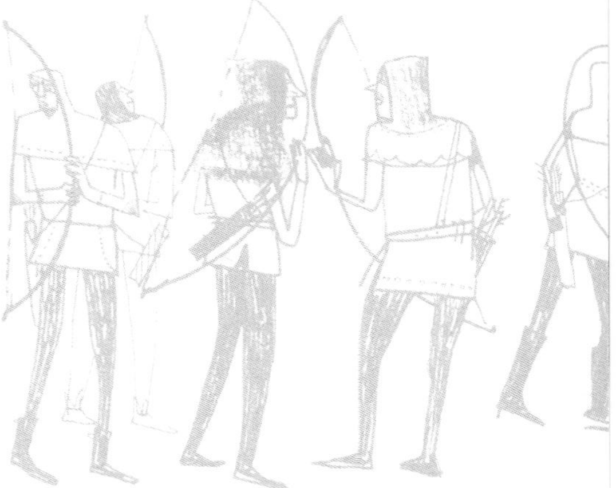

The Scots were battle-hardened and high in confidence, but numbered fewer than 10,000 in total. There were some archers and perhaps 500 light horse, but the army consisted almost entirely of men on foot armed with spears, axes and swords.

They gathered in the ancient forest known as the Torwood, between Stirling Castle and the advancing English army. But Bruce was still not committed to fight, and on Saturday 22 June he withdrew to the New Park, another wooded area half a mile north of the Bannock Burn, just beside the Kirkton of St Ninians.

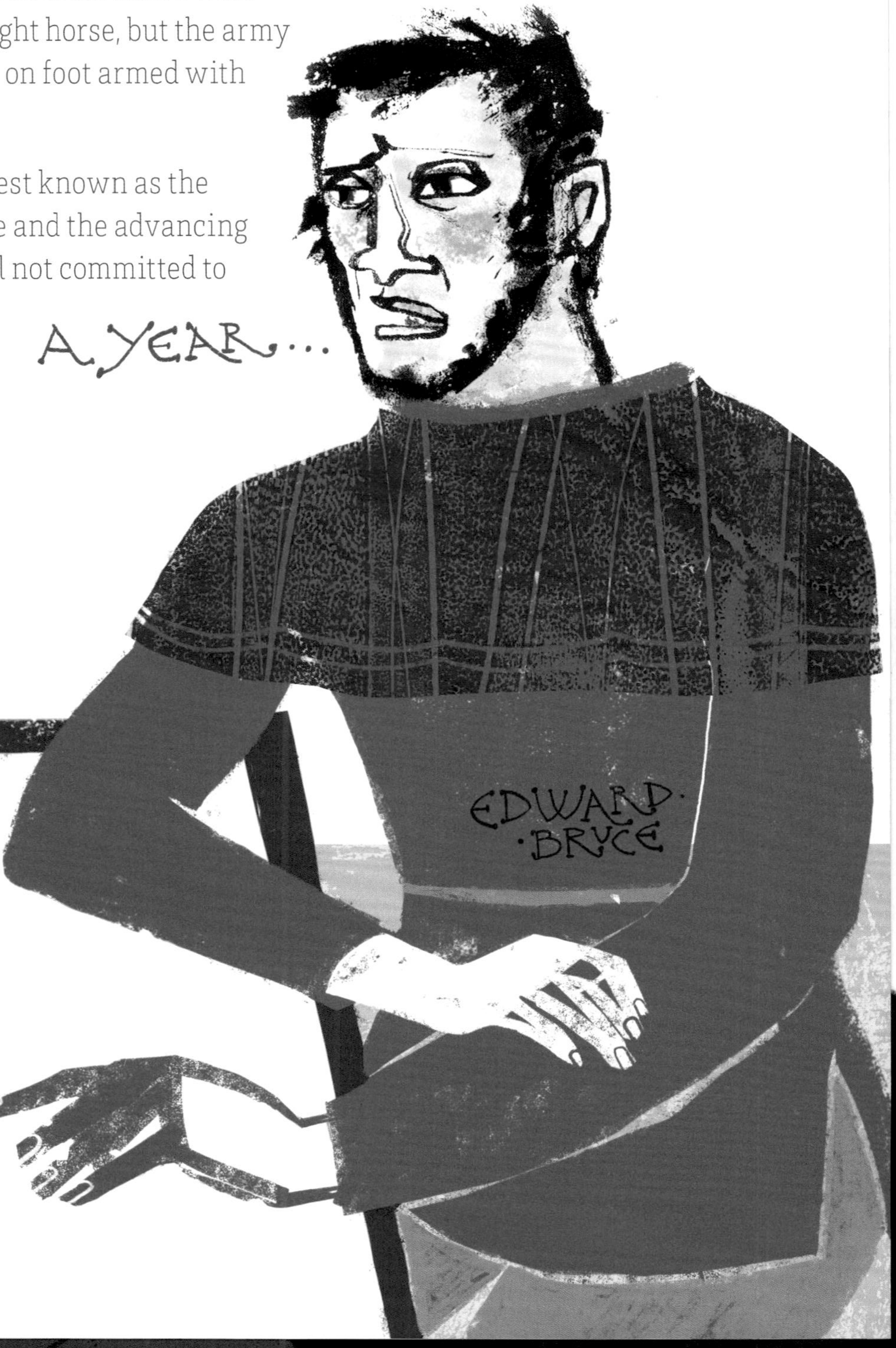
A YEAR...
EDWARD BRUCE

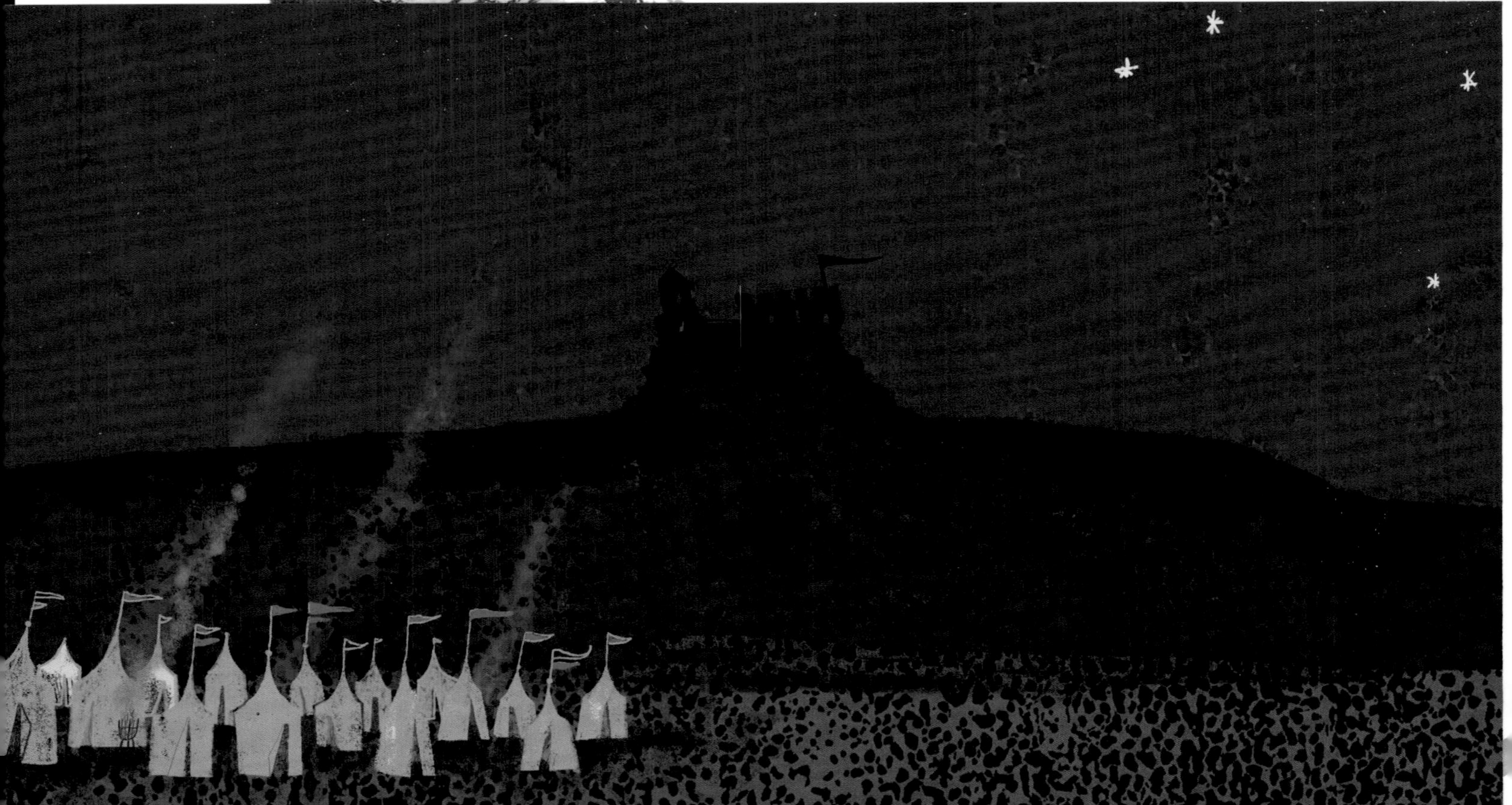

Bruce considered quitting while he had the advantage, but during the night a Scots knight in the enemy camp, Sir Alexander Seton, came over with news that the English were thoroughly disheartened. Using planks and doors taken from local houses to build makeshift bridges, they had withdrawn across the Bannock Burn to protect themselves against a surprise attack, and now they lay beneath the stars, exhausted but awake and fearful. Bruce held a council of war, and his closest friends and commanders agreed that, this time, they should stand and fight.

On the Monday morning, the English moved back to the higher ground to face the Scots, but were hemmed in on three sides by the Bannock Burn and its tributaries. The Scots had undoubtedly had the more restful night. According to John Barbour in his epic poem *The Bruce*, written 60 years later, their King addressed them thus: 'We have three advantages over our foes. First, right is on our side, and God will always fight for what is right. Second, they bring with them such riches that if we are victorious even the poorest among you will be a wealthy man.

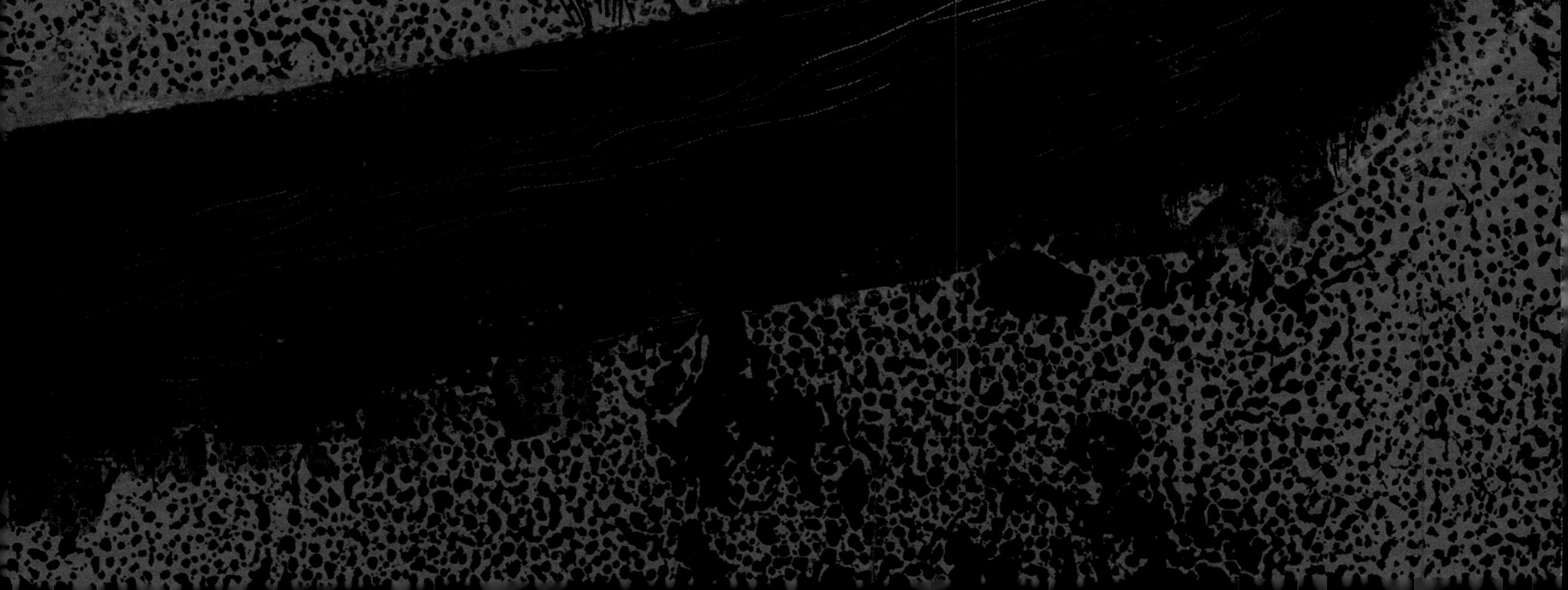

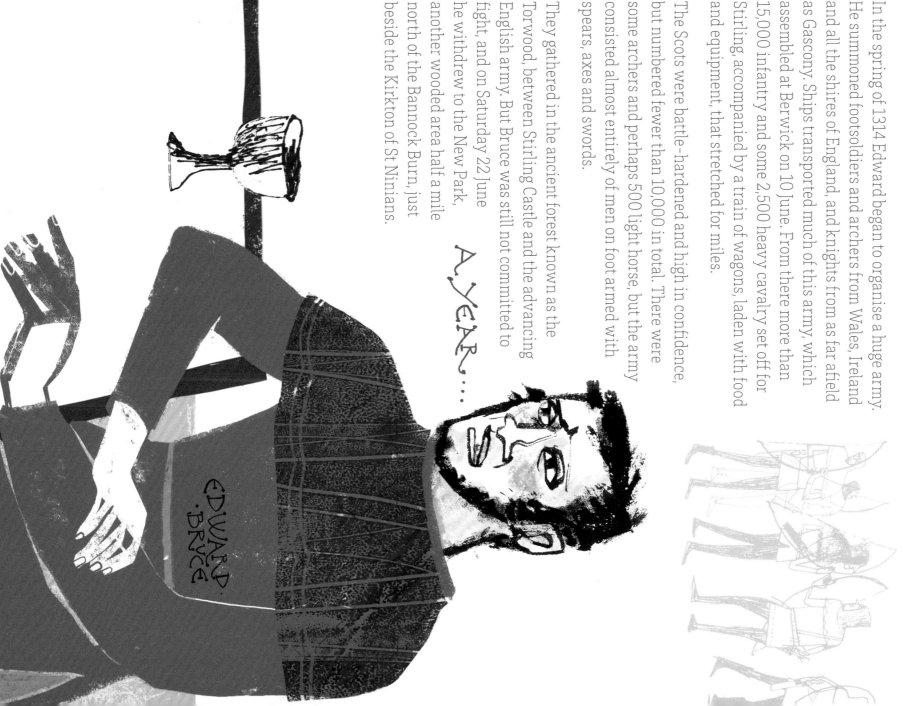

In the spring of 1314 Edward began to organise a huge army. He summoned footsoldiers and archers from Wales, Ireland and all the shires of England, and knights from as far afield as Gascony. Ships transported much of this army, which assembled at Berwick on 10 June. From there more than 15,000 infantry and some 2,500 heavy cavalry set off for Stirling, accompanied by a train of wagons, laden with food and equipment, that stretched for miles.

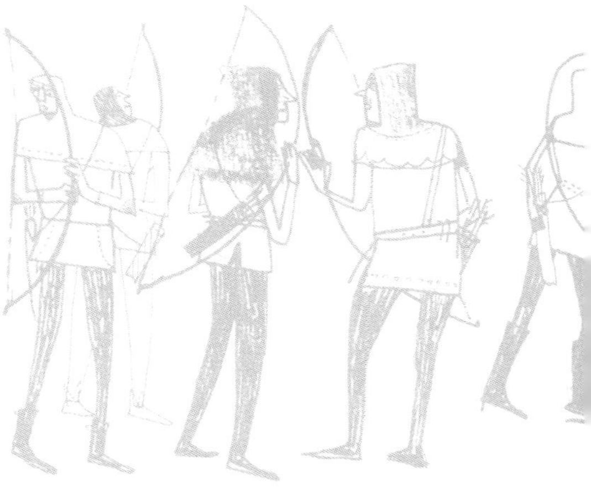

The Scots were battle-hardened and high in confidence, but numbered fewer than 10,000 in total. There were some archers and perhaps 500 light horse, but the army consisted almost entirely of men on foot armed with spears, axes and swords.

They gathered in the ancient forest known as the Torwood, between Stirling Castle and the advancing English army. But Bruce was still not committed to fight, and on Saturday 22 June he withdrew to the New Park, another wooded area half a mile north of the Bannock Burn, just beside the Kirkton of St Ninians.

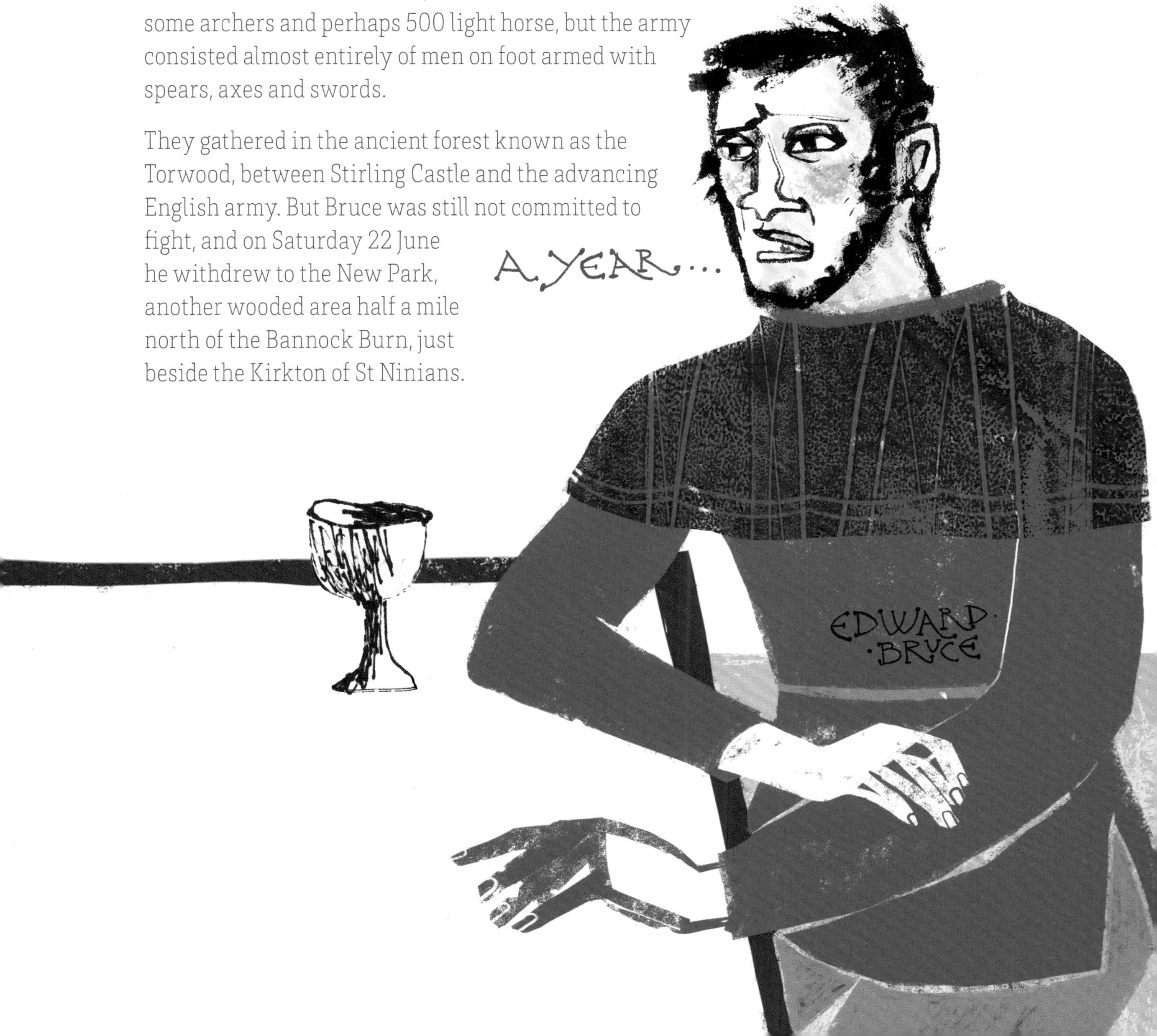
A YEAR...
EDWARD BRUCE

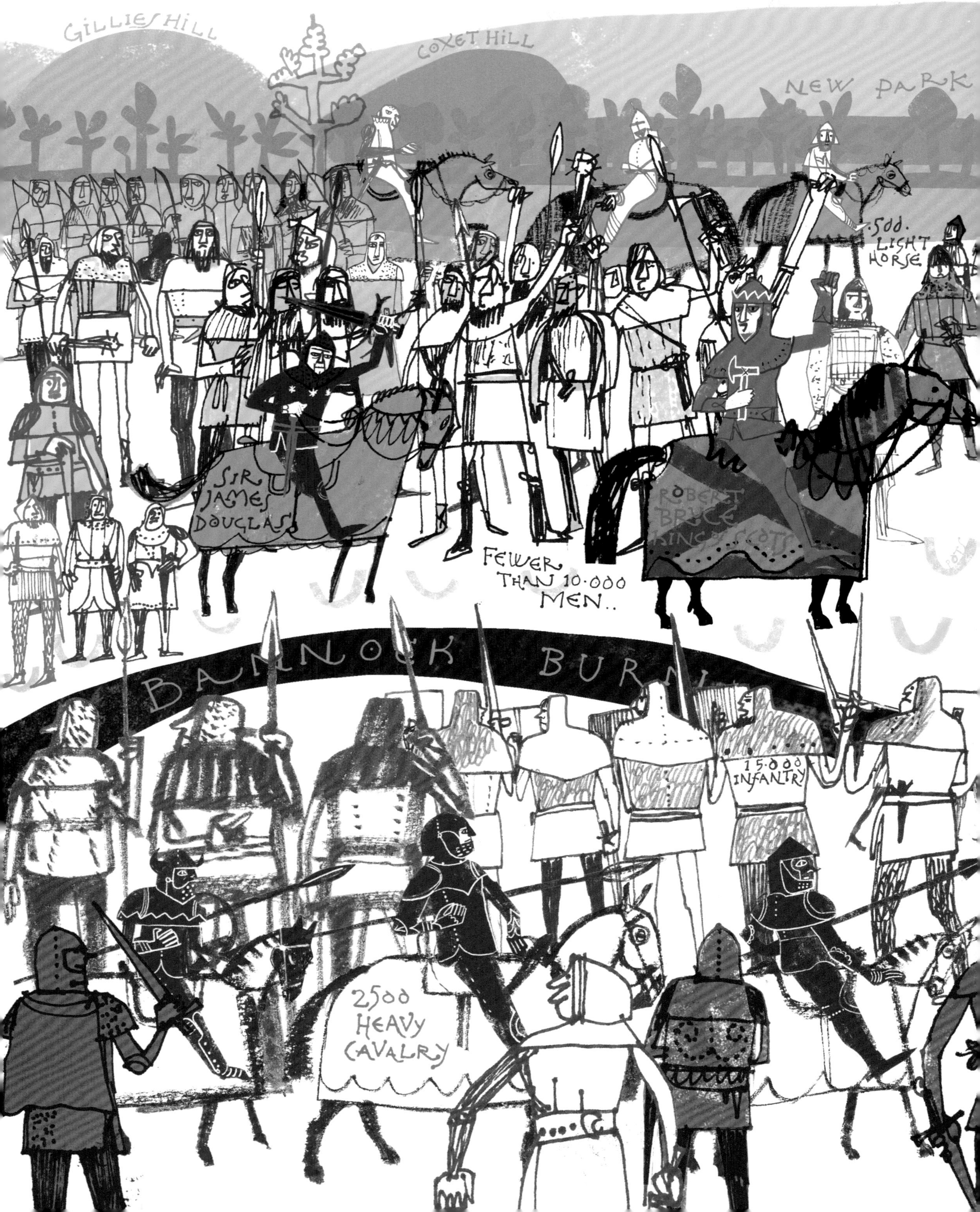
GILLIES HILL
COXET HILL
NEW PARK
500 LIGHT HORSE
SIR JAMES DOUGLAS
ROBERT BRUCE KING of SCOTS
FEWER THAN 10.000 MEN..
BANNOCK BURN
15.000 INFANTRY
2500 HEAVY CAVALRY

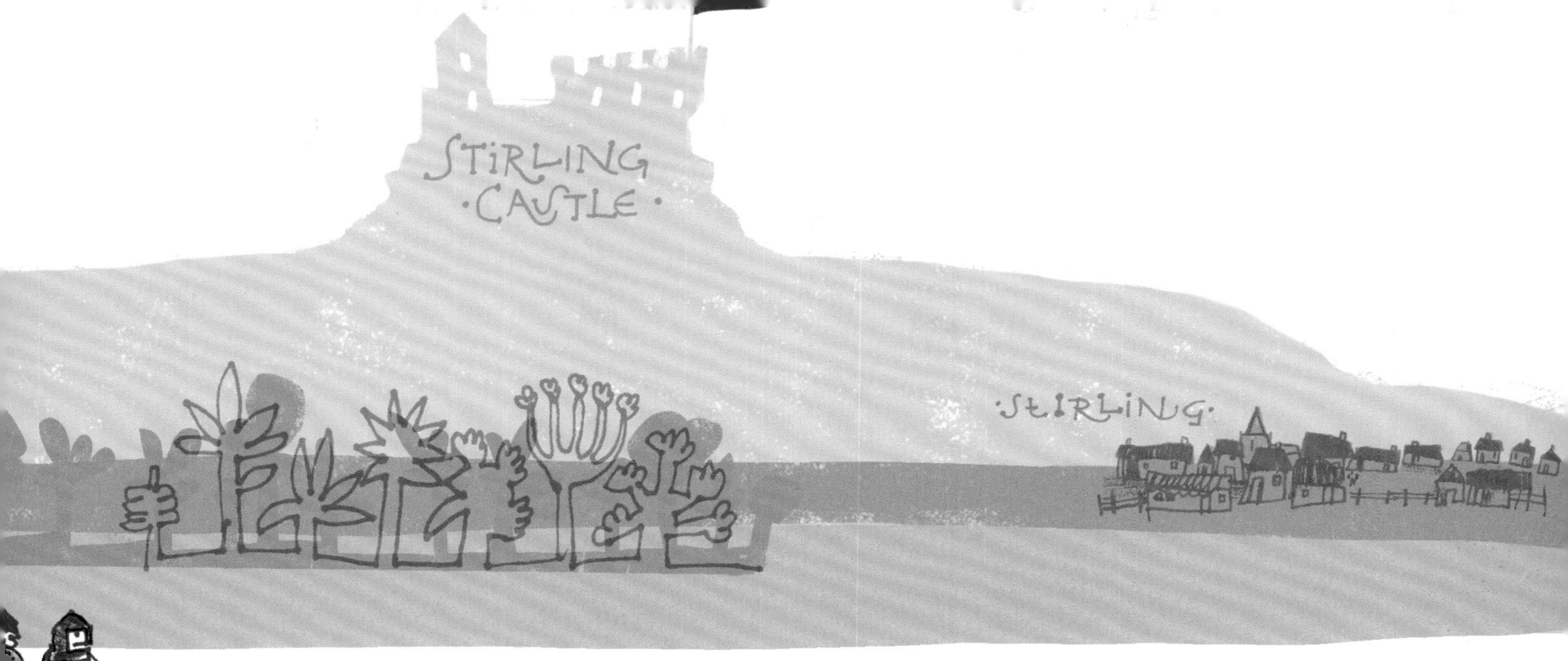
STIRLING CASTLE
STIRLING

The Scottish army was now in a strong defensive position: the road to Stirling went through St Ninians; to the east lay the Carse – low-lying, boggy land interspersed with steep-banked burns; to reach Stirling the English army would have to pass between the Scots and this difficult terrain.

To narrow the route further, the Scots honeycombed the ground on either side of the road with 'pots' – holes a foot in diameter and knee-deep – and disguised them with sticks and grass. Then they waited for the English to advance.

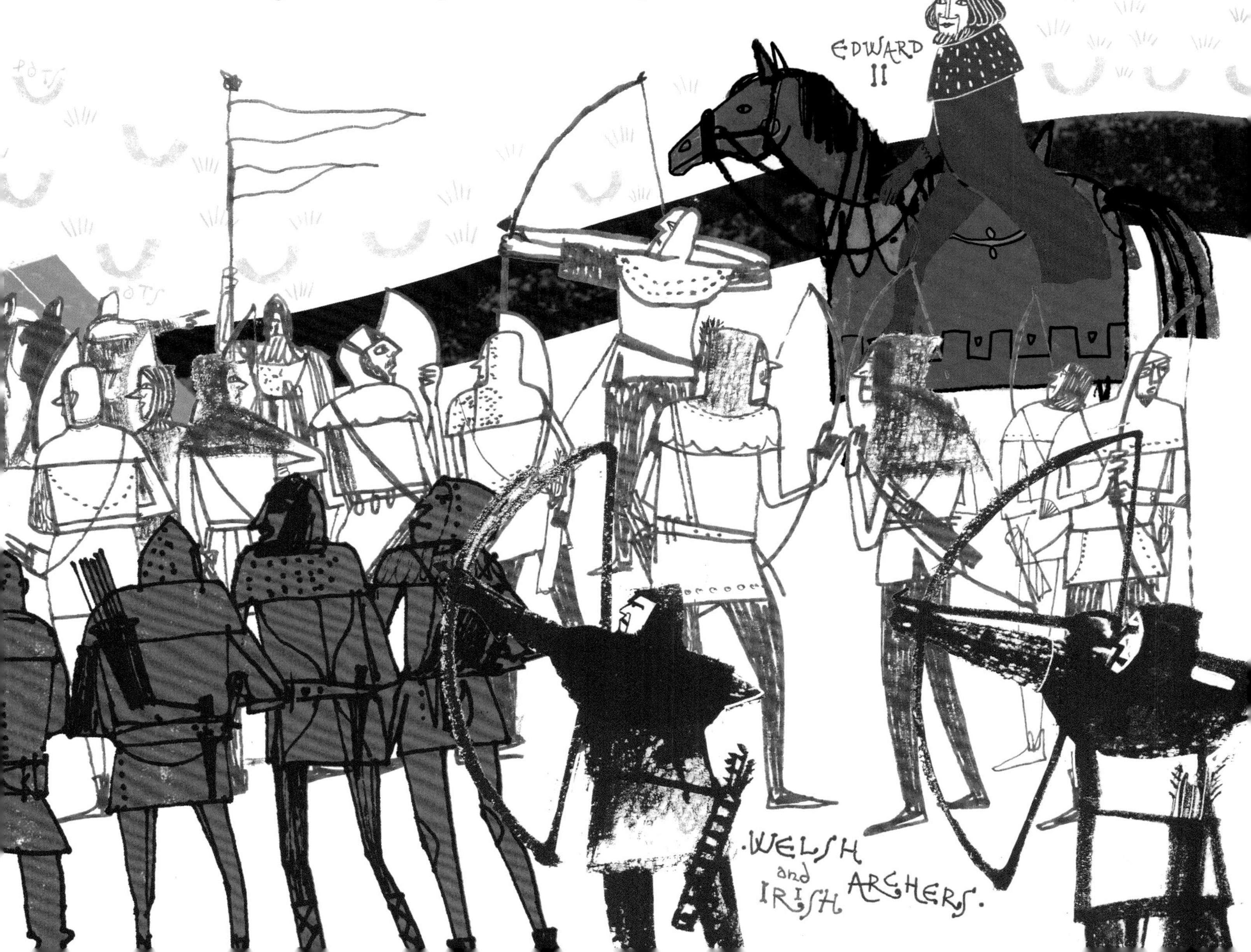
The CARSE
POTS
EDWARD II
WELSH and IRISH ARCHERS.

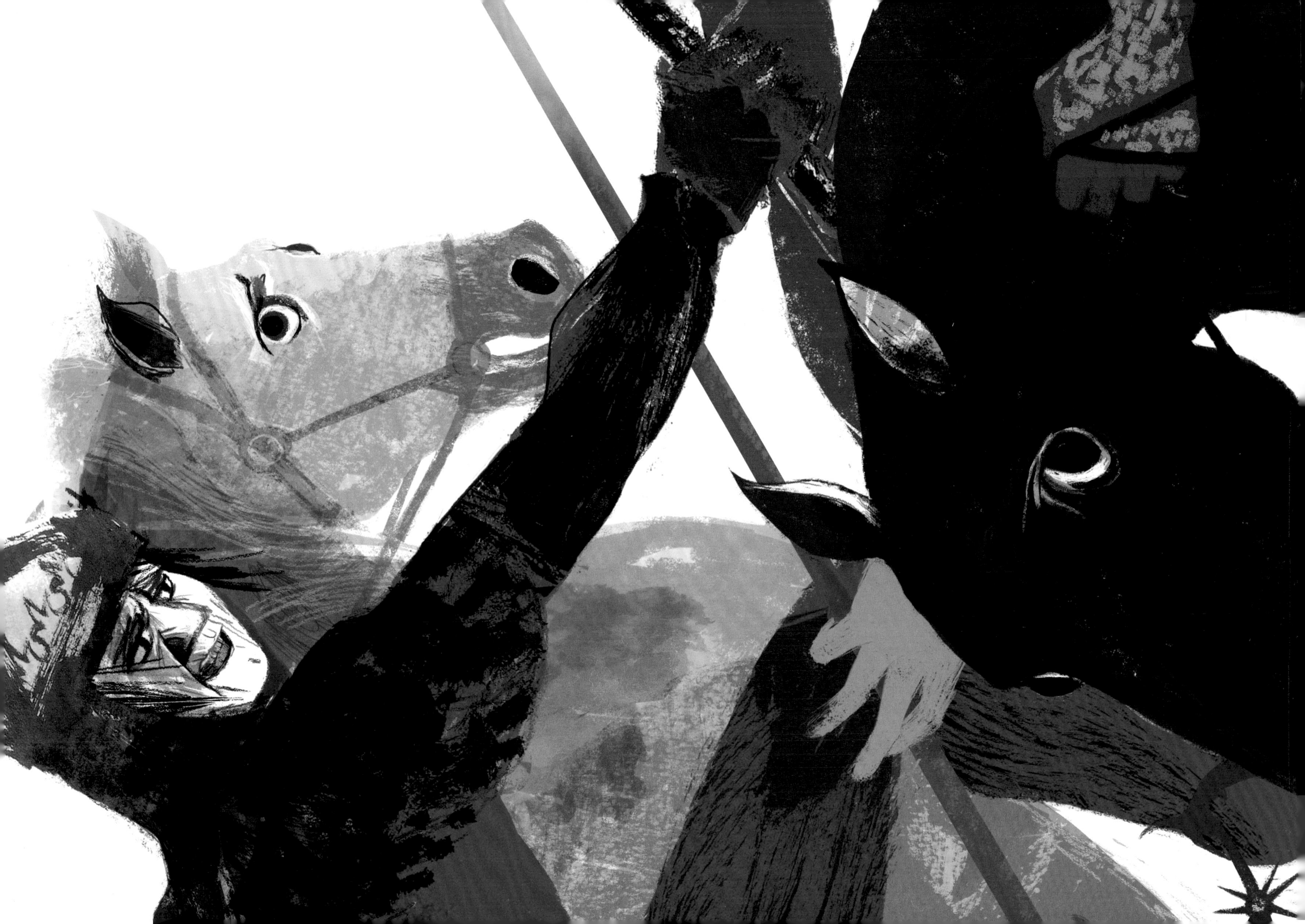

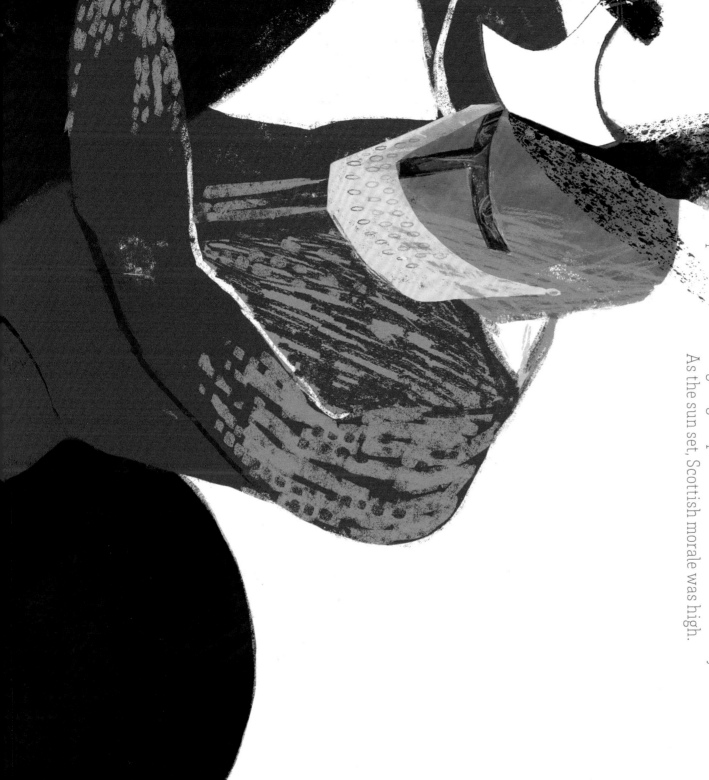

Sunday 23 June dawned dry and sunny. A large contingent of English cavalry pressed forward on the Scottish positions. Among these knights was one Sir Henry de Bohun, who spied a lone figure in front of the enemy lines, mounted on a grey pony, armed with an axe and wearing a high-crowned helmet – Bruce himself! De Bohun spurred his warhorse forward, eager for glory, levelling his lance at the King. Bruce pulled his mount clear of the charge, stood in his stirrups and swung his axe down, splitting open not only de Bohun's helmet but also his head. The blow shattered the handle of the axe, much to the King's displeasure. The Scots, hugely encouraged by this episode, surged forward and forced the English cavalry to withdraw.

Meanwhile, another squadron of English horse was attempting to make its way to the castle between the road and the Carse. Thomas Randolph, the Earl of Moray, rapidly blocked them with a large number of soldiers formed into a schiltron, and a fierce and bloody fight ensued. Without the support of bowmen, the English could not penetrate this hedgehog of spears and retreated with heavy losses.

As the sun set, Scottish morale was high.

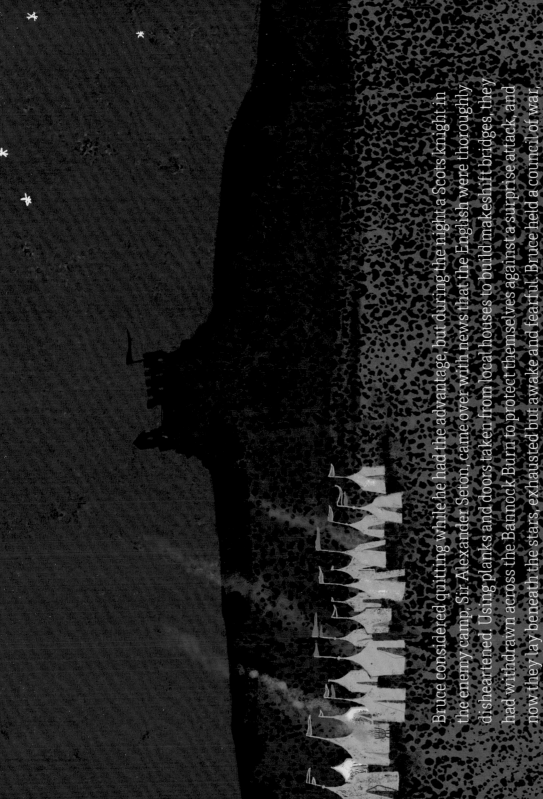

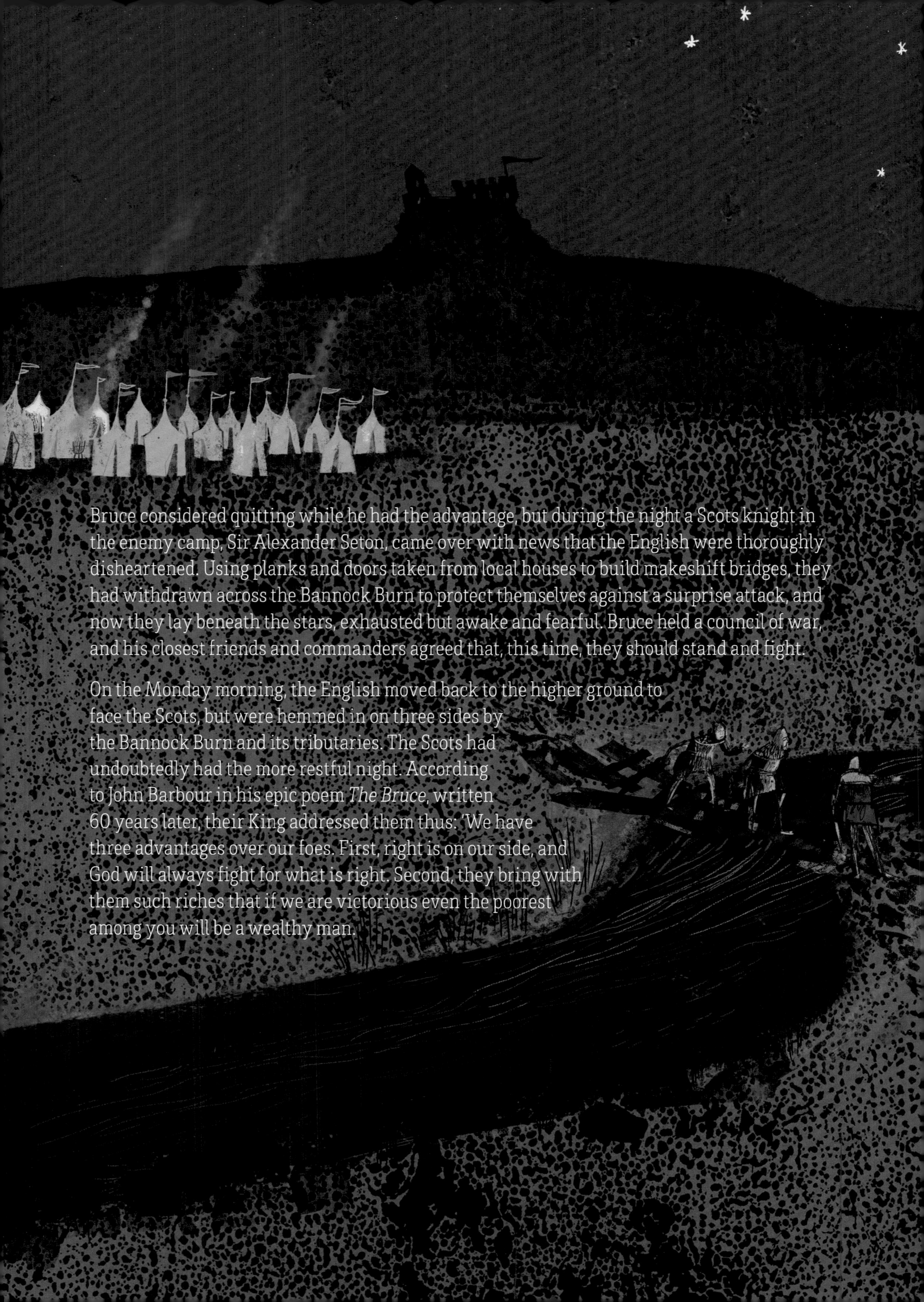

Bruce considered quitting while he had the advantage, but during the night a Scots knight in the enemy camp, Sir Alexander Seton, came over with news that the English were thoroughly disheartened. Using planks and doors taken from local houses to build makeshift bridges, they had withdrawn across the Bannock Burn to protect themselves against a surprise attack, and now they lay beneath the stars, exhausted but awake and fearful. Bruce held a council of war, and his closest friends and commanders agreed that, this time, they should stand and fight.

On the Monday morning, the English moved back to the higher ground to face the Scots, but were hemmed in on three sides by the Bannock Burn and its tributaries. The Scots had undoubtedly had the more restful night. According to John Barbour in his epic poem *The Bruce*, written 60 years later, their King addressed them thus: 'We have three advantages over our foes. First, right is on our side, and God will always fight for what is right. Second, they bring with them such riches that if we are victorious even the poorest among you will be a wealthy man.'

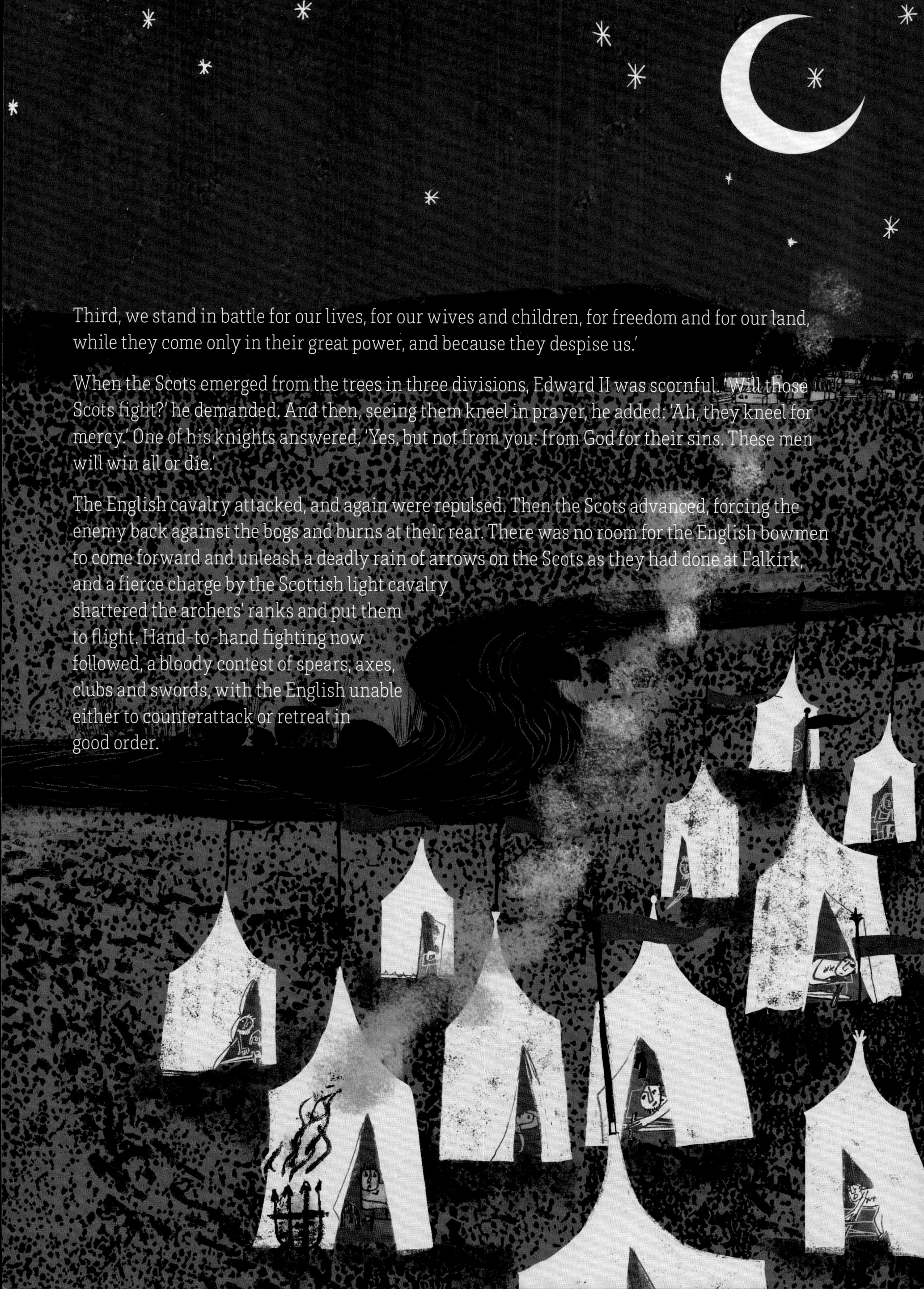

Third, we stand in battle for our lives, for our wives and children, for freedom and for our land, while they come only in their great power, and because they despise us.'

When the Scots emerged from the trees in three divisions, Edward II was scornful. 'Will those Scots fight?' he demanded. And then, seeing them kneel in prayer, he added: 'Ah, they kneel for mercy.' One of his knights answered, 'Yes, but not from you: from God for their sins. These men will win all or die.'

The English cavalry attacked, and again were repulsed. Then the Scots advanced, forcing the enemy back against the bogs and burns at their rear. There was no room for the English bowmen to come forward and unleash a deadly rain of arrows on the Scots as they had done at Falkirk, and a fierce charge by the Scottish light cavalry shattered the archers' ranks and put them to flight. Hand-to-hand fighting now followed, a bloody contest of spears, axes, clubs and swords, with the English unable either to counterattack or retreat in good order.

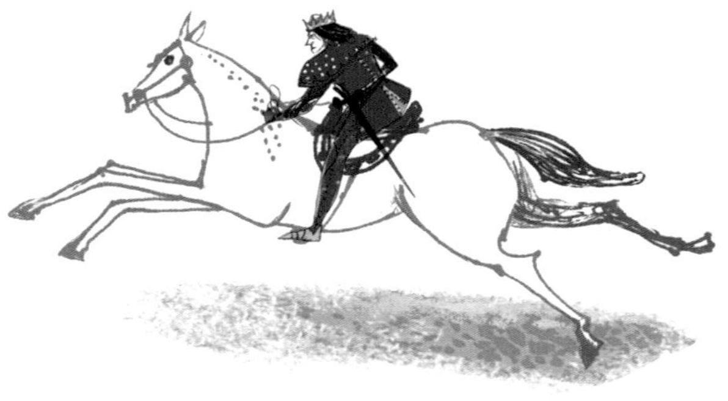

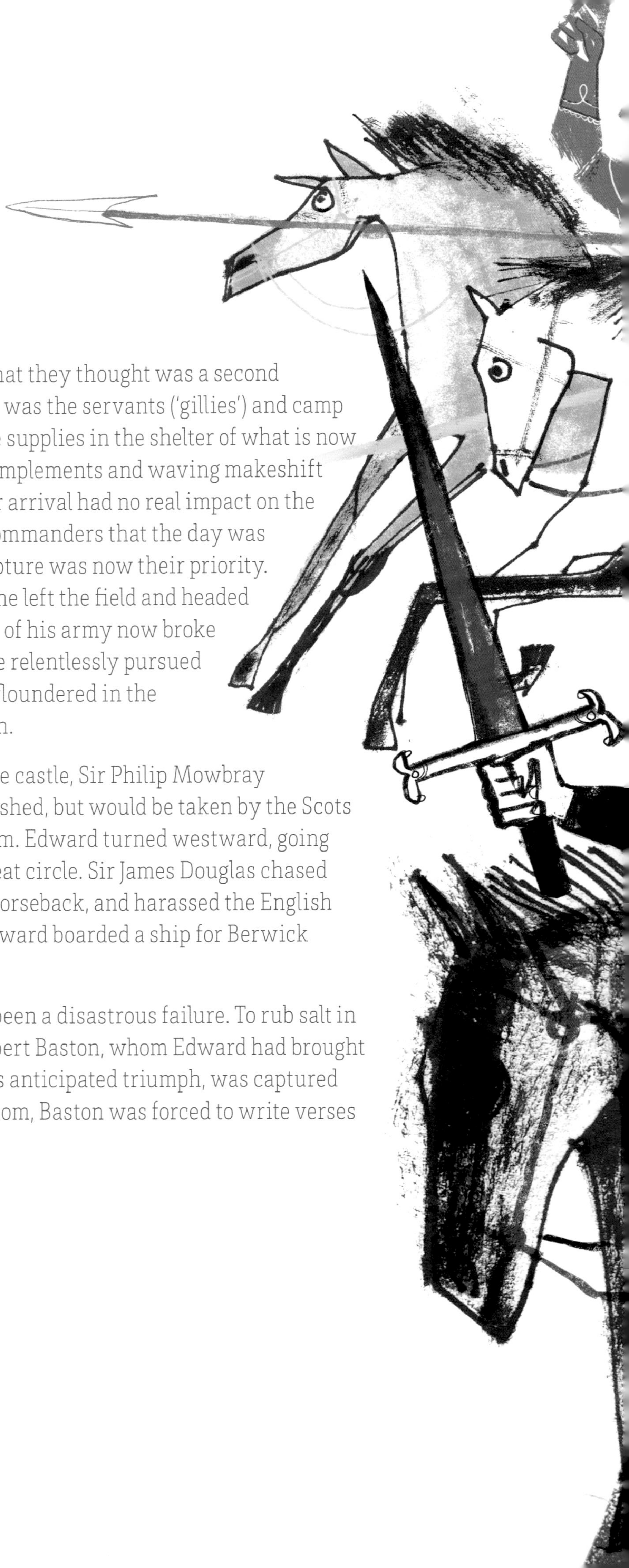

As their despair increased, they saw what they thought was a second Scottish army approaching. In fact, this was the servants ('gillies') and camp followers who had been left to guard the supplies in the shelter of what is now called Gillies Hill. Armed with kitchen implements and waving makeshift banners, they swarmed into view. Their arrival had no real impact on the battle, except to persuade the English commanders that the day was lost. To save Edward II from death or capture was now their priority. Five hundred knights protected him as he left the field and headed for the safety of Stirling Castle. The rest of his army now broke and fled, north, east and south, and were relentlessly pursued by the Scots. Many were killed as they floundered in the muddy ditch that was the Bannock Burn.

When Edward and his party reached the castle, Sir Philip Mowbray advised him that he could enter if he wished, but would be taken by the Scots when the castle was surrendered to them. Edward turned westward, going round behind the Scottish army in a great circle. Sir James Douglas chased after him with a force of sixty men on horseback, and harassed the English knights all the way to Dunbar. There Edward boarded a ship for Berwick and safety.

His attempt to reconquer Scotland had been a disastrous failure. To rub salt in the wound, a Carmelite friar named Robert Baston, whom Edward had brought north to compose a poem celebrating his anticipated triumph, was captured by the Scots. In order to regain his freedom, Baston was forced to write verses glorifying *their* victory.

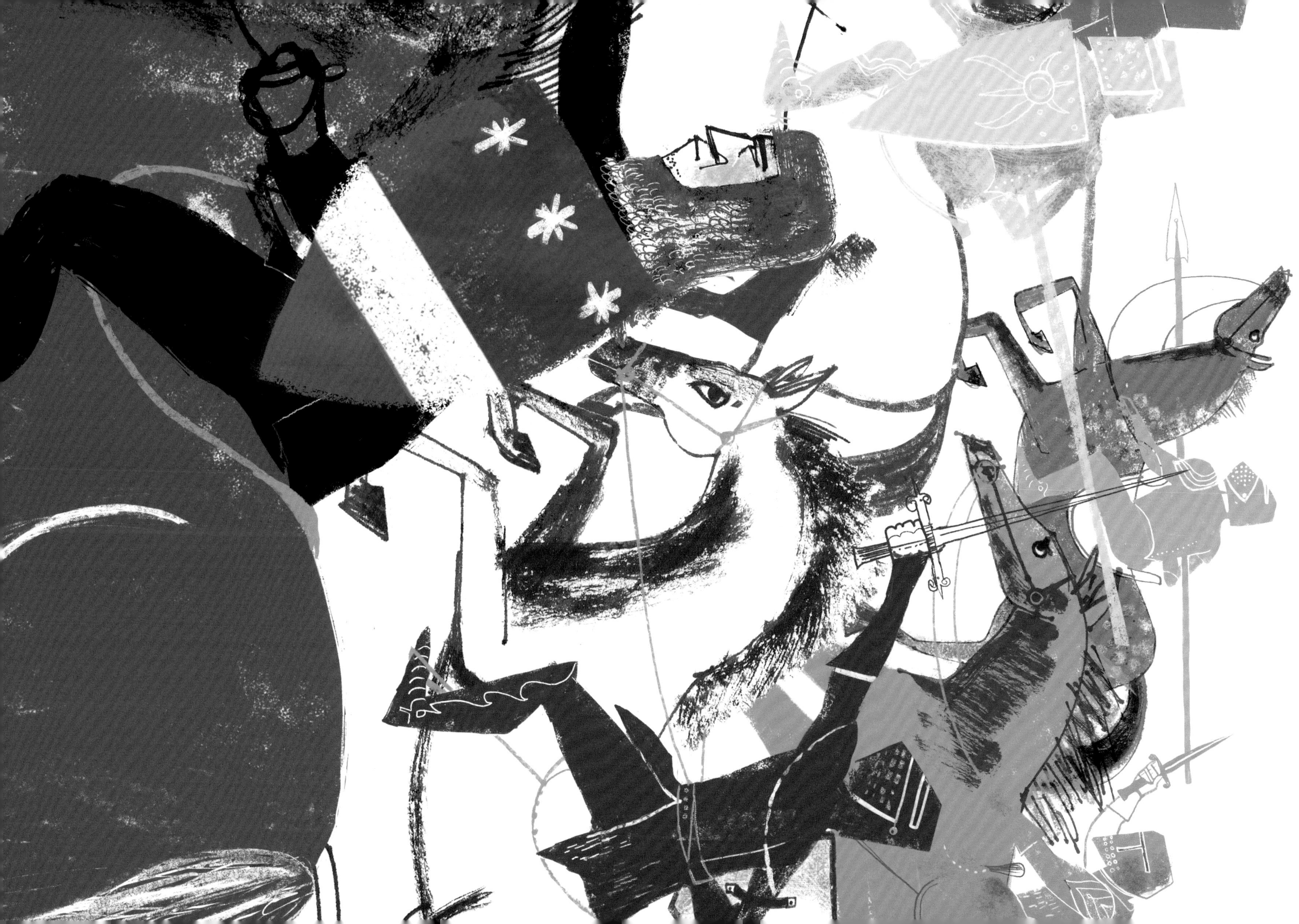

The Battle of Bannockburn sealed Robert the Bruce's authority in Scotland, and secured his country's independence. It would be many years, however, before the English would formally acknowledge this, and those years were marked by much cross-Border warfare. Bruce also carried the conflict to Ireland, trying to build a united front against England, but this project was ultimately unsuccessful, as the Irish were scarcely more favourable to Scottish influence than they were to that of the English.

At home, Robert proved himself a strong and clever monarch, who brought internal stability and prosperity to his country. And he made continuous diplomatic efforts to gain international recognition, especially that of the Papacy, for Scotland as a free and separate nation.

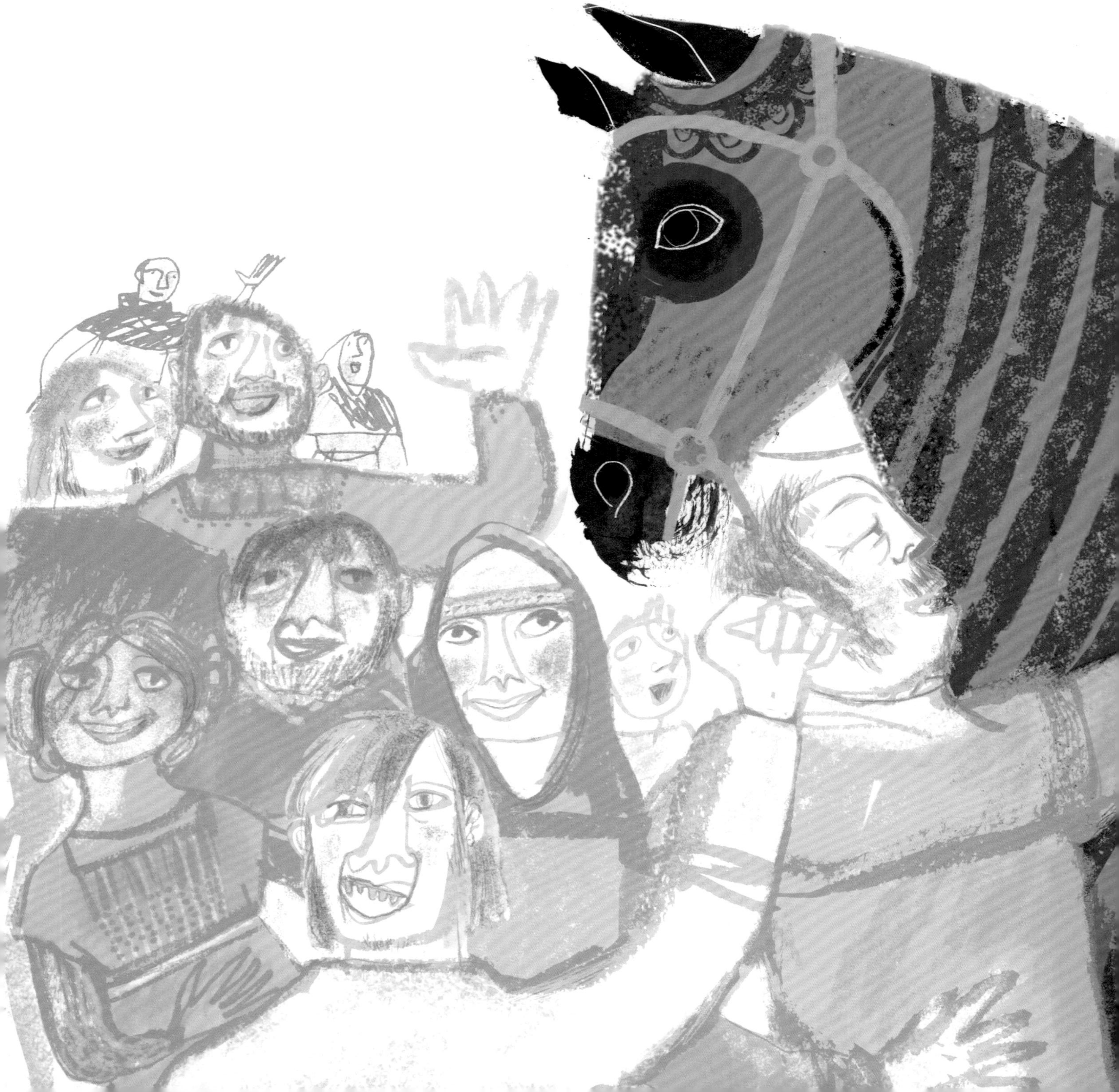

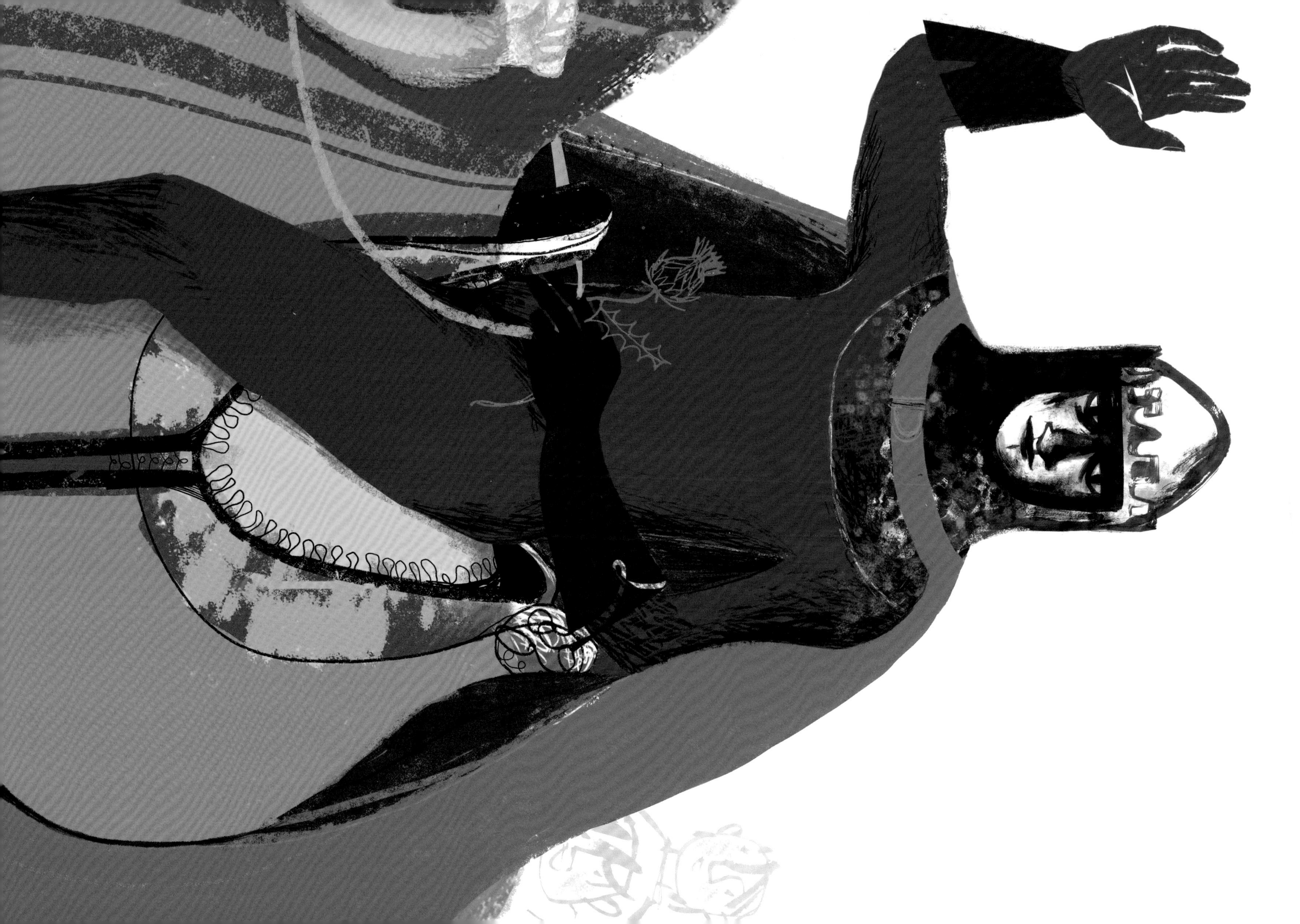

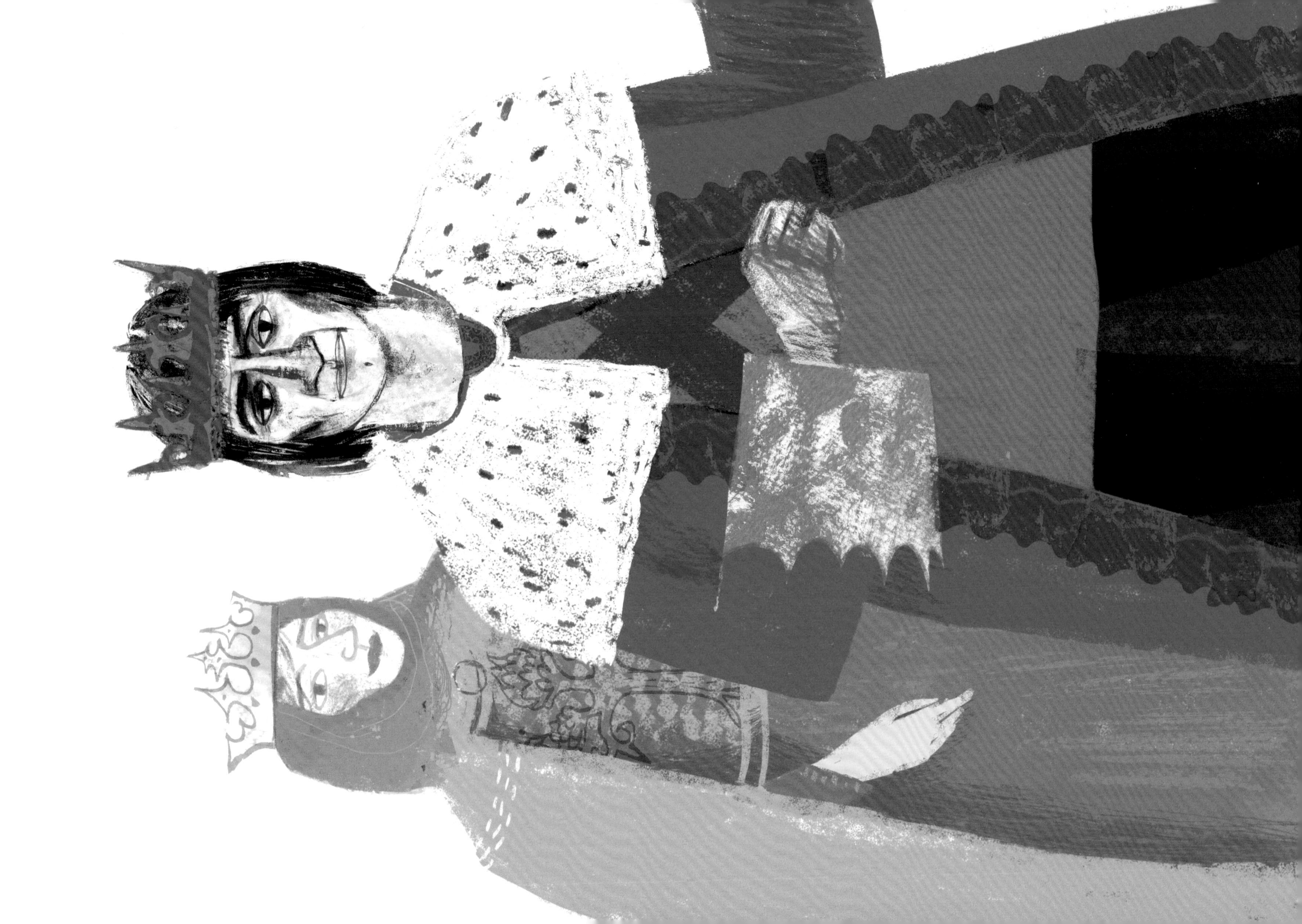

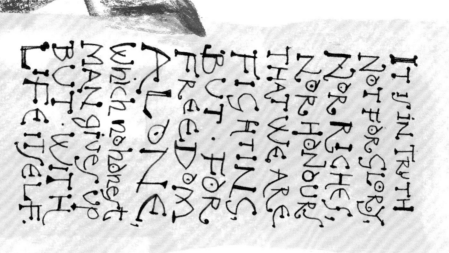

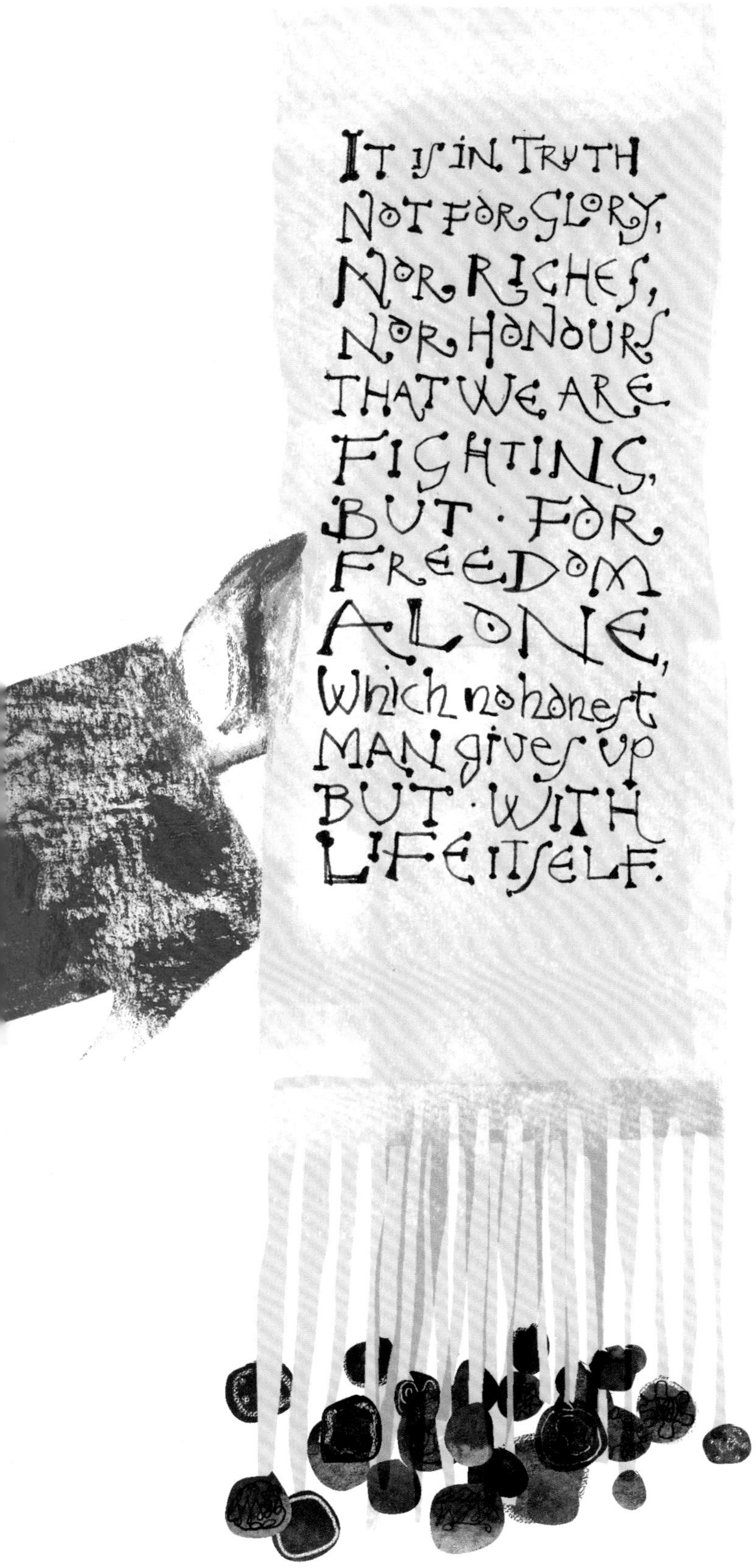

IT IS IN TRUTH
NOT FOR GLORY,
NOR RICHES,
NOR HONOURS
THAT WE ARE
FIGHTING,
BUT FOR
FREEDOM
ALONE,
Which no honest
MAN gives up
BUT WITH
LIFE ITSELF.

Six years after Bannockburn, in 1320, the barons of Scotland wrote a letter, known today as the Declaration of Arbroath, to Pope John XXII. It is a stirring assertion of Scottish freedom and independence, and it specifically acknowledges the efforts of King Robert in achieving those ends. But, it famously goes on, should the King abandon the principles for which he fought, and consent to subject the kingdom or its people to English rule,

... we should exert ourselves at once to drive him out as our enemy and a subverter of his own right and ours, and make some other man who was well able to defend us our King; for, as long as a hundred of us remain alive, never will we on any conditions be subjected to the lordship of the English. It is in truth not for glory, nor riches, nor honours that we are fighting, but for freedom alone, which no honest man gives up but with life itself.

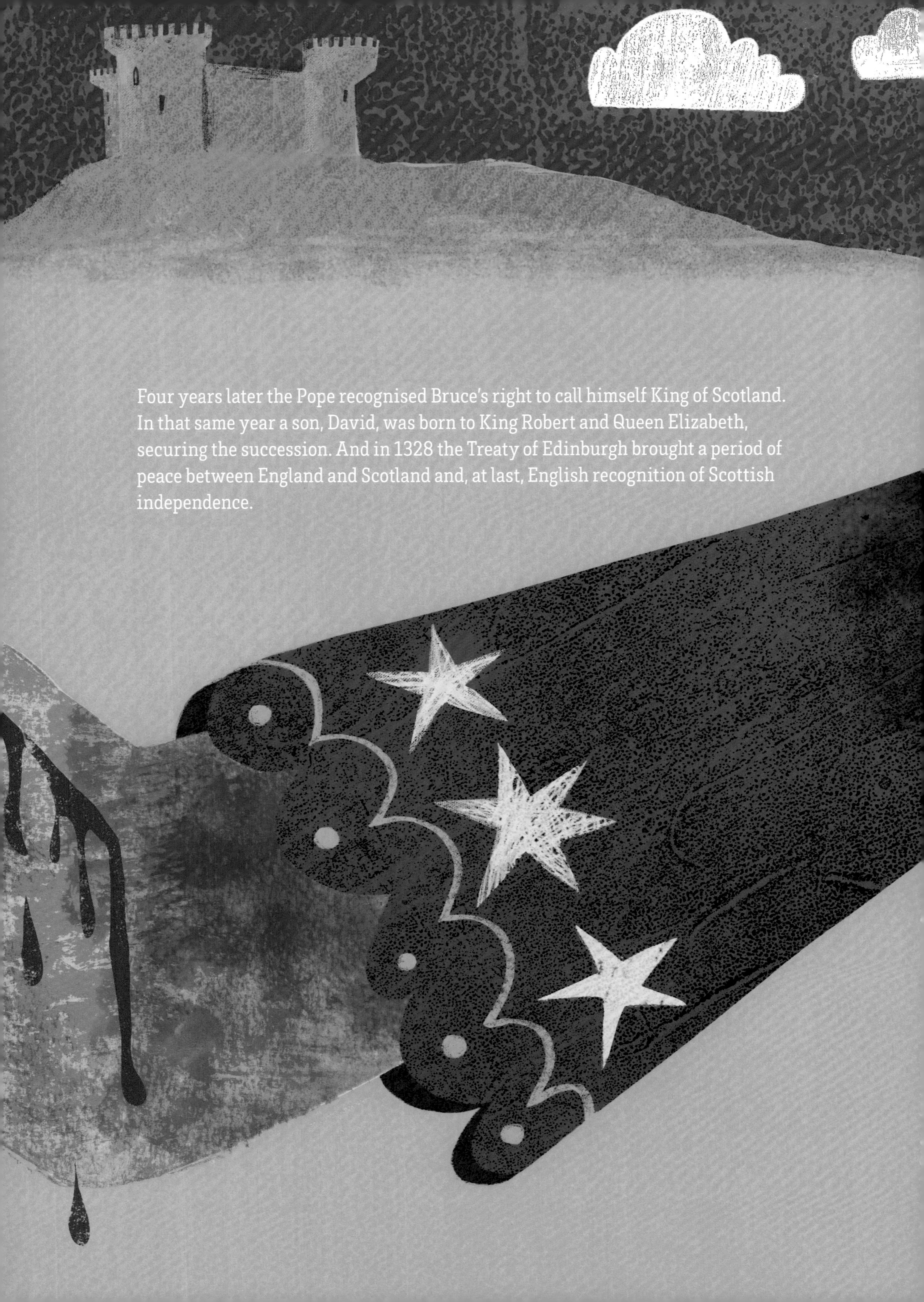

Four years later the Pope recognised Bruce's right to call himself King of Scotland. In that same year a son, David, was born to King Robert and Queen Elizabeth, securing the succession. And in 1328 the Treaty of Edinburgh brought a period of peace between England and Scotland and, at last, English recognition of Scottish independence.

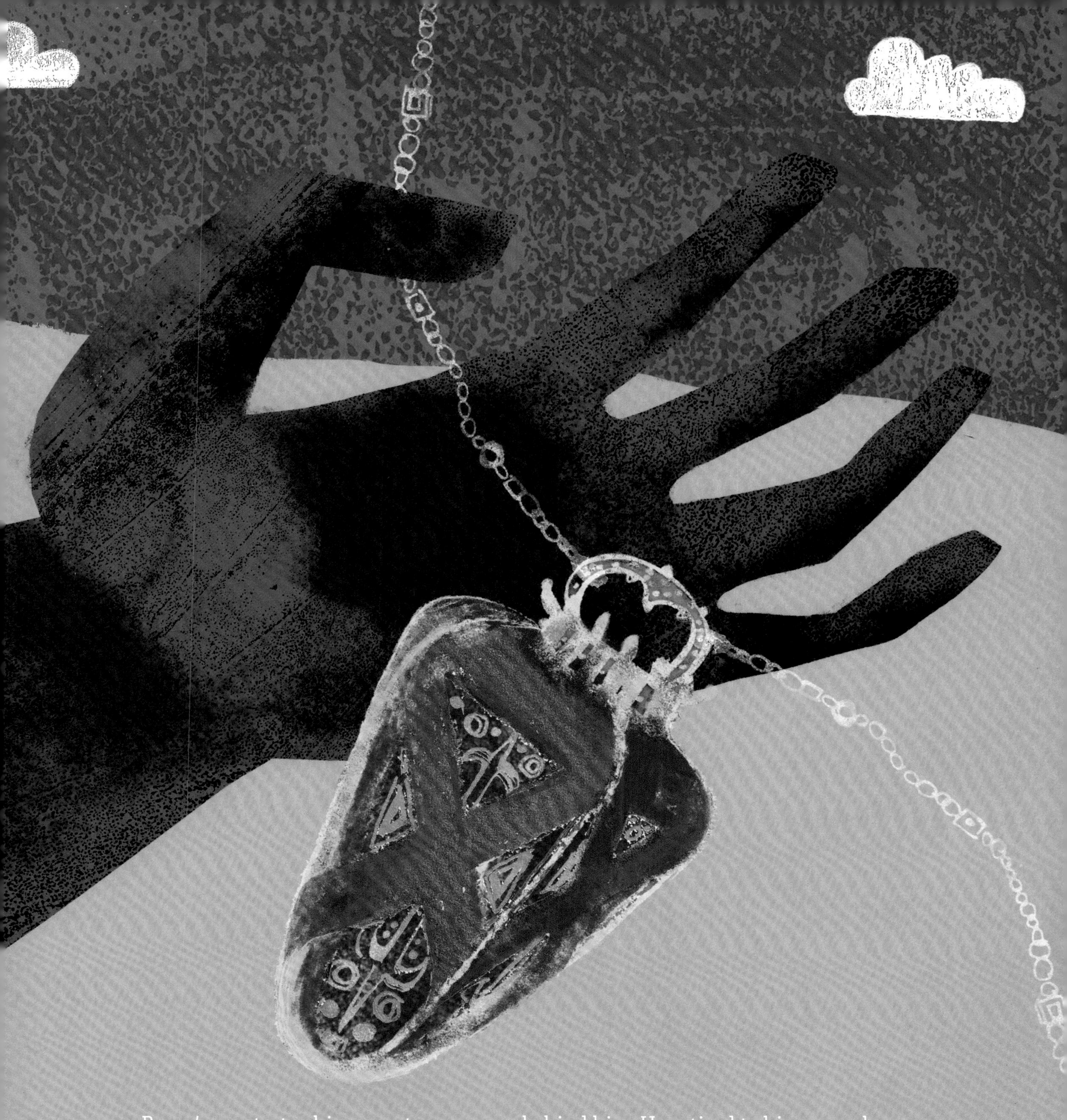

Bruce's greatest achievements were now behind him. He retired to his manor house at Cardross and there, possibly suffering from leprosy, he died at the age of fifty-five. Lamented by his people, he was buried at Dunfermline Abbey, but he left instructions that his heart should be taken on a crusade against the enemies of the Christian God. Accordingly, his loyal friend Sir James Douglas carried the heart in a casket to Spain, where he was killed fighting the Moors. Bruce's heart was brought back to Scotland and interred at Melrose Abbey.

Robert the Bruce is one of the great heroic figures of medieval Europe. His story is also the story of his country. When he fought for Scotland's freedom he also fought for his own interests. But without his personal ambition and careful planning, Bruce would not have succeeded where another hero, William Wallace, had failed. Wallace lit the torch of Scottish liberty; Bruce carried it triumphantly to victory. In doing so he forged the Scots into a nation. They even found the language for expressing this shared sense of identity, declaring that they could, if King Robert betrayed their hard-won independence, remove him from the throne and put another in his place. That strong belief and principle – that sovereignty lies not with one individual or institution but with the people – has been deeply felt by the Scots from Bruce's times to the present, and has helped to form the Scottish character.

It is now 700 years since the victory which secured his kingship and the independence of the nation. It is unlikely that Bruce's name will be soon forgotten.

First published in 2014 by
Birlinn Ltd
West Newington House
10 Newington Road
Edinburgh
EH9 1QS

www.birlinn.co.uk

ISBN: 978 1 78027 183 5

The right of James Robertson to be identified as the author of this work has been asserted by her in accordance with the Copyright, Designs and Patents Act, 1988

British Library Cataloguing-in-Publication Data
A catalogue record for this book is available on request from the British Library

Conceived and art directed by James Hutcheson

Typeset in HvD Brix Slab

Printed and bound by Proost NV, Belgium

The publisher acknowledges investment from Creative Scotland towards the publication of this volume

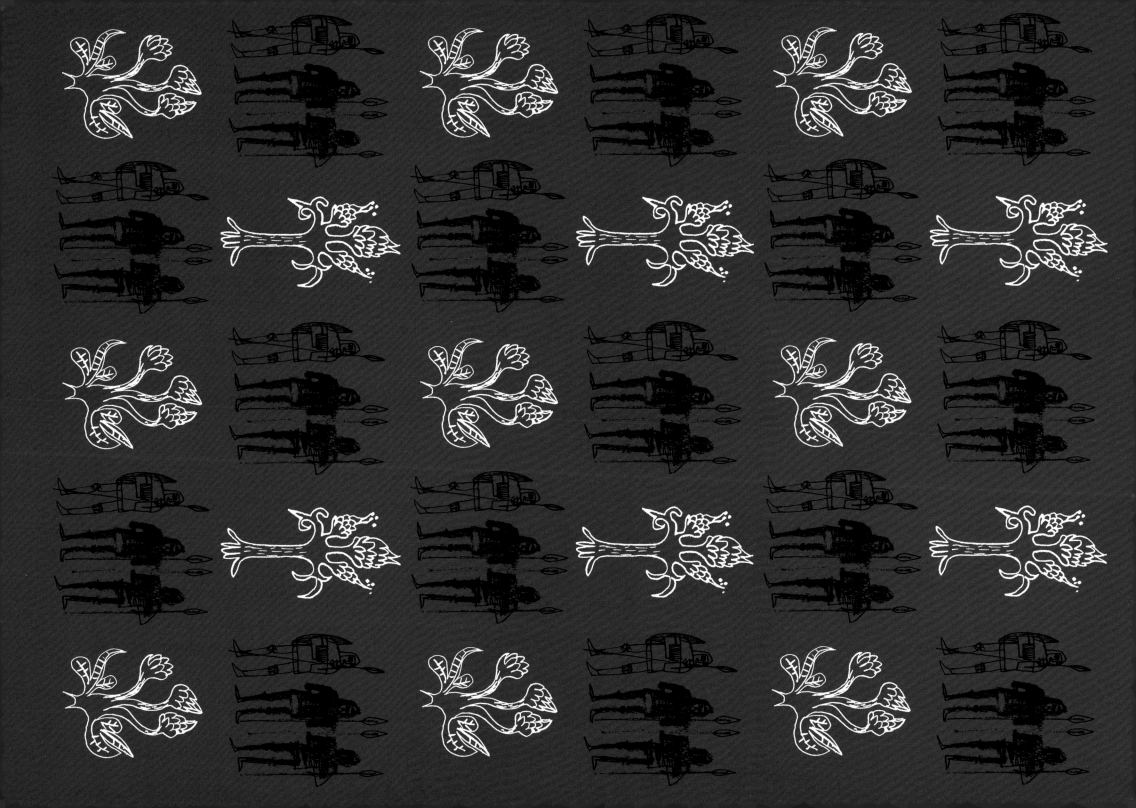

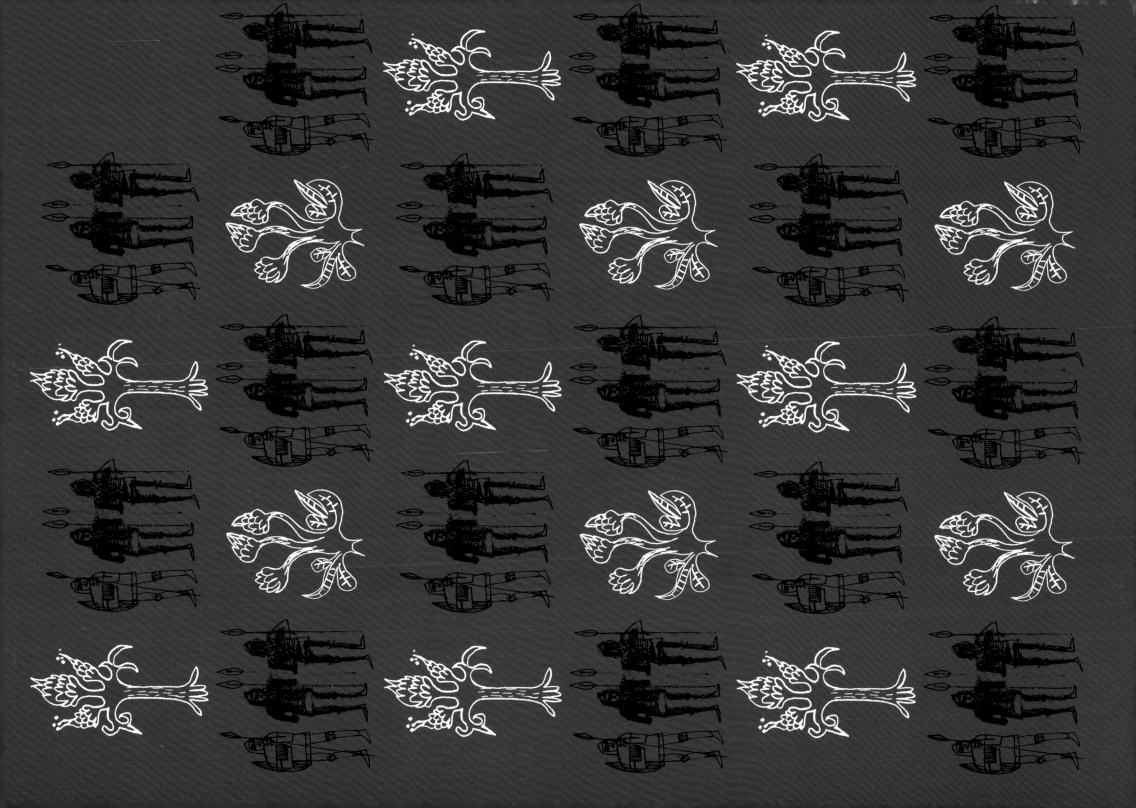